The Naming of America

Martin Waldseemüller's 1507 World Map and the *Cosmographiae Introductio*

In Memory of David Woodward and J. Brian Harley ... whose writings taught us not only how to look, but what to look for.

The Naming of America

Martin Waldseemüller's 1507 World Map and the *Cosmographiae Introductio*

Featuring a new translation and commentary by
John W. Hessler, Geography and Map Division, Library of Congress

"Although it is very difficult if not impossible in this life to achieve certainty about these questions, at the same time it is utterly feeble not to use every effort in testing the available theories, or to leave off before we have considered them in every way, and come to the end of our resources."

Plato, *Phaedo* 84d

Copyright © 2008 The Library of Congress

First published in 2008 by GILES
An imprint of D Giles Limited
2nd Floor
162-164 Upper Richmond Road,
London SW15 2SL, UK
www.gilesltd.com

ISBN: 978-1-904832-49-2

For The Library of Congress:
Director of Publishing: W. Ralph Eubanks
Editor and Managing Editor: Aimee Hess
Photography by Lee Ewing

For D Giles Limited:
Copy-edited and proof-read by Bernard Dod
Designed by Bark Media, London
Produced by GILES, an imprint of D Giles Limited, London
Printed and bound in Hong Kong

Library of Congress Cataloging-in-Publication Data

Waldseemüller, Martin, 1470-1521?
[Cosmographiae introductio. English]
  The naming of America : Martin Waldseemuller's 1507 world map and the
Cosmographiae introductio / featuring a new translation and commentary
by John W. Hessler.
    p. cm.
  Published in association with the Library of Congress.
  ISBN 978-1-904832-49-2
  1. America--Name--Early works to 1800. 2. America--Discovery and
exploration--Early works to 1800. 3. Geography--Early works to 1800. 4.
 Cartography--Early works to 1800. 5. America--Early accounts to 1600.
6. Waldseemüller, Martin, 1470-1521? Cosmographiae introductio. 7.
America--Discovery and exploration--Maps. 8. World maps. 9. Early
maps. 10. Vespucci, Amerigo, 1451-1512. I. Hessler, John W. II.
Library of Congress. III. Title.
  E125.V6W1513 2007
  970.01--dc22

                                               2007043126

Contents

Acknowledgments

My work on the 1507 World Map and related projects surrounding the Waldseemüller map corpus began five years ago and has been supported by many individuals, foundations and research libraries. First and foremost on this list is Dr. John Hébert, Chief of the Geography and Map Division of the Library of Congress. John has not only given me many hours of conversation about the Waldseemüller maps but also allowed me to avail myself of his vast knowledge of early Spanish and Portuguese cartography. His knowledge of these subjects has shortened my research time in many places and his support of my work on this project and on my other publications and mathematical modeling of the 1507 map has been invaluable.

At the Library of Congress I would like to express my sincere thanks to several colleagues who with their encouragement have helped and supported this project, especially Heather Wanser, Senior Paper Conservator at the LOC, and Jim Flatness, Curator in the Geography and Map Division. Many people read and commented on the translation including Ann Grossman, Paper Conservator at the LOC, Kirsten Seaver, Fellow of the Royal Geographic Society and Aimee Hess and Ralph Eubanks from the Library's Publishing Office. Also at the Library of Congress I would thank Arthur Dunkleman, Curator of the J. Kislak Collection, for his support in all things Waldseemüller, and Mr. J. Kislak for giving me open access to the 1516 Carta Marina and the remaining parts of the Schöner Sammelbund.

When I was struggling to comprehend Johannes Schöner's contorted paleography Dr. Owen Gingerich of Harvard University helped me with several difficult attributions and provided me with much-needed examples of Schöner's handwriting from his astrological notebooks. I would also like to thank the staff of the manuscript collections at the Österreichische Nationalbibliothek in Vienna and the Hill Monastic Library for hunting down many of the volumes of Johannes Schöner's extant library. For financial support I would also like to express my sincere appreciation to the Friends of J.B. Harley Foundation and to the National Science Foundation for their generous fellowships that allowed me to travel to Budapest and Vienna in 2005. I also must acknowledge the family of Martin Gray whose generous grant to the Library of Congress has made this publication possible.

Finally, to paraphrase Anthony Grafton, I owe a vast debt to Waldseemüller himself. He has given me many years of frustration and amusement, led me to dozens of texts and problems which I would not otherwise have explored, and offered me a tortuous but fascinating path into the complex, cluttered mental world of the early sixteenth century.

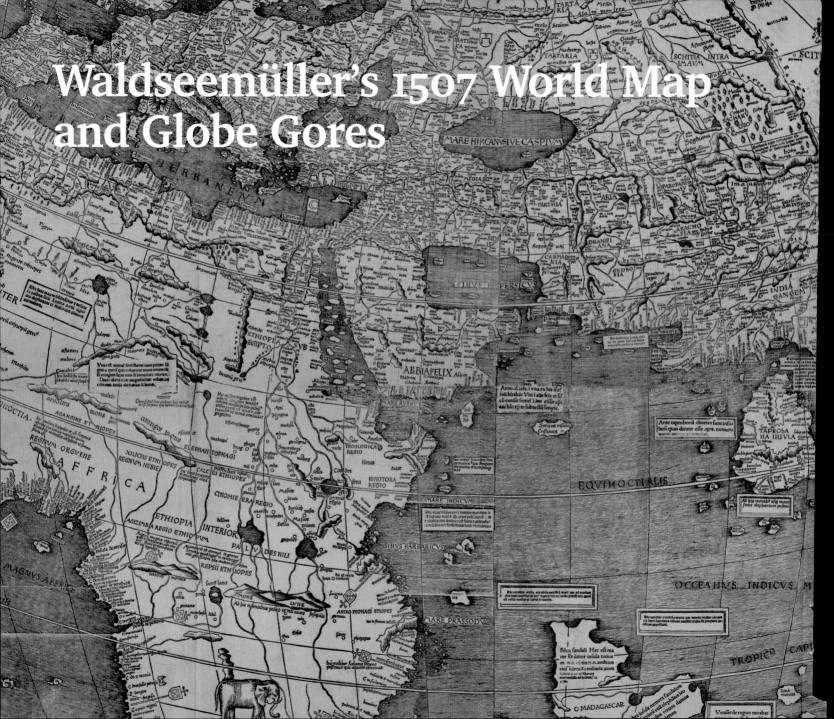

Waldseemüller's 1507 World Map and Globe Gores

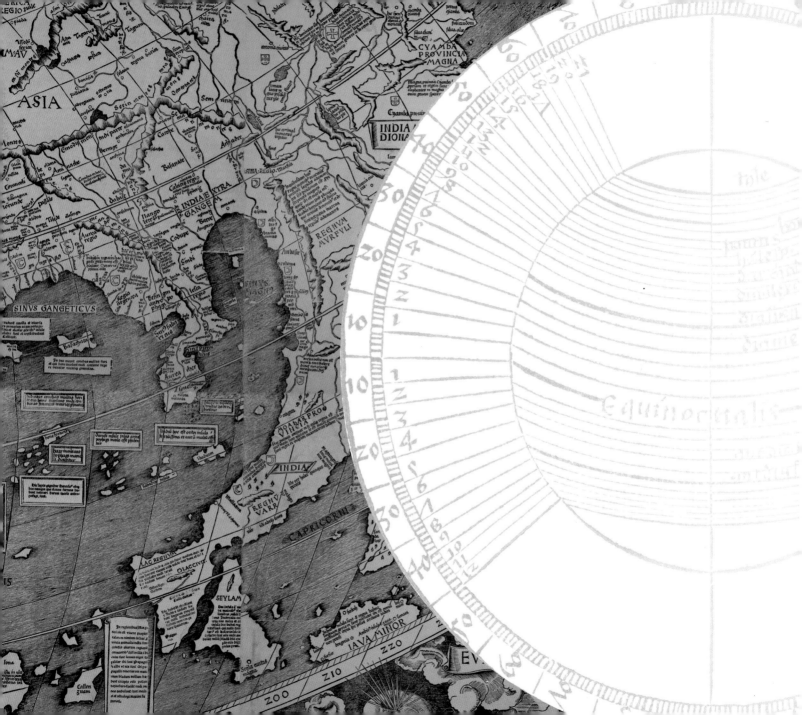

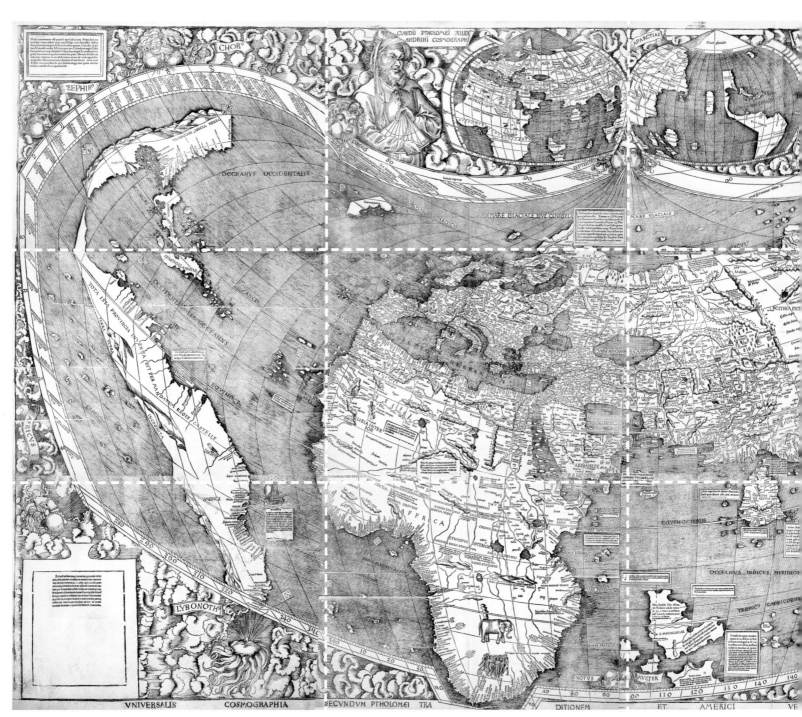

UNIVERSALIS   COSMOGRAPHIA   SECVNDVM PTHOLOMAEI TRA   DITIONEM   ET   AMERICI   VE

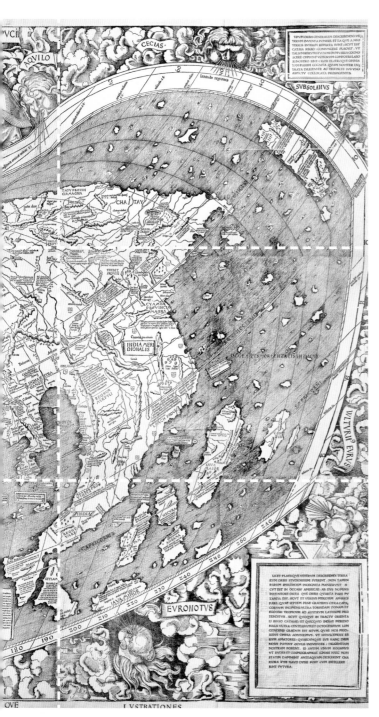

Fig 1. _____

This figure shows a composite view of Waldseemüller's 1507 World Map displayed as a wall map much in the way it might have been by Waldseemüller's patrons. Few wall maps survive from this period and perhaps the best evidence for how they were treated in the early 16th century comes from Lorenz Fries' booklet *Uslegung der Mercarthen oder Carta Marina,* written around 1525 as a guide to his reduced version of Waldseemüller's 1516 Carta Marina. Fries' text reads:

If you want to mount the map sheets as one map for your own use and glue it in place securely, take some linen or some piece of clean cloth and place a firm board on a table or chest and stretch the sheet firmly by hammering nails all around the border. Next cut the pages of the map along the left or right side so that they fit next to each other without spaces. The middle sheets must also be cut lengthwise along the top and bottom. You should first definitely try to fit the sheets together before you begin to glue. After you have checked the positioning put some glue, but not too strong, into a small pan or pot. Warm it up, but not too hot. Then take a brush, one that is not too small but one that has soft hairs. Brush the back of the first sheet with glue and place it on the upper left. Employ an assistant so you can move fast and place the pages down so that they fit immediately. After the sheet is down put a clean paper over it and rub it with a piece of cloth until it is smooth.

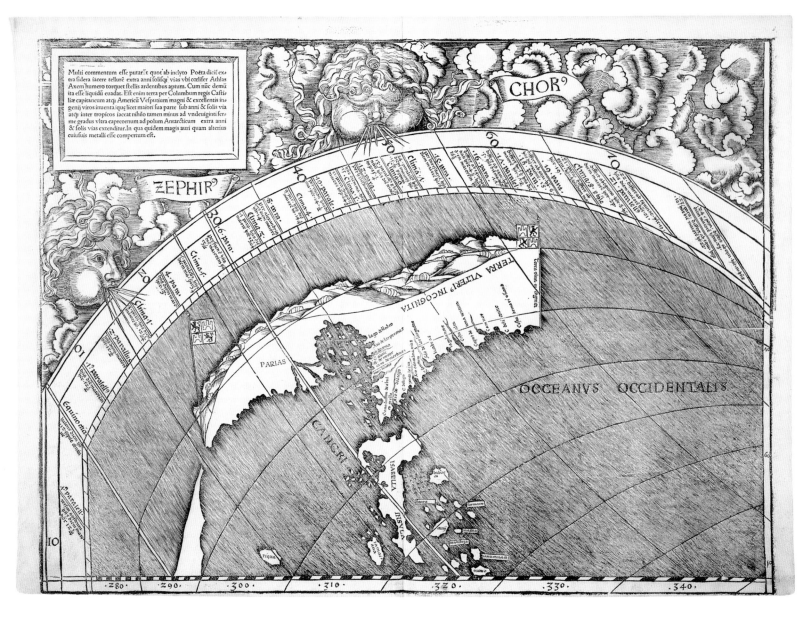

Sheet 1.

The upper text block on this sheet of the map mentions the role of both Columbus and Vespucci in the discovery of the New World. The text reads:

Many have regarded as an invention the words of a famous poet that "beyond the stars lies a land, beyond the path of the year and the sun, where Atlas, who supports the heavens, revolves on his shoulders the axis of the world, set with gleaming stars," but now finally it proves clearly to be true. For there is a land, discovered by Columbus, a captain of the King of Castile, and by Americus Vespucius, both men of very great ability, which, though in great part it lies beneath "the path of the year and of the sun" and between the tropics, nevertheless extends about 19 degrees beyond the Tropic of Capricorn toward the Antarctic Pole, "beyond the path of the year and the sun." Here a greater amount of gold has been found than of any other metal.

Sheet 2.

This sheet shows the continent of South America separated from Asia, revealing a new ocean. The sheet also contains a region around the Canary Islands that shows obvious changes having been made to the woodblocks. These can be seen by looking closely at the linear and polygonal separations that surround this area on the map.

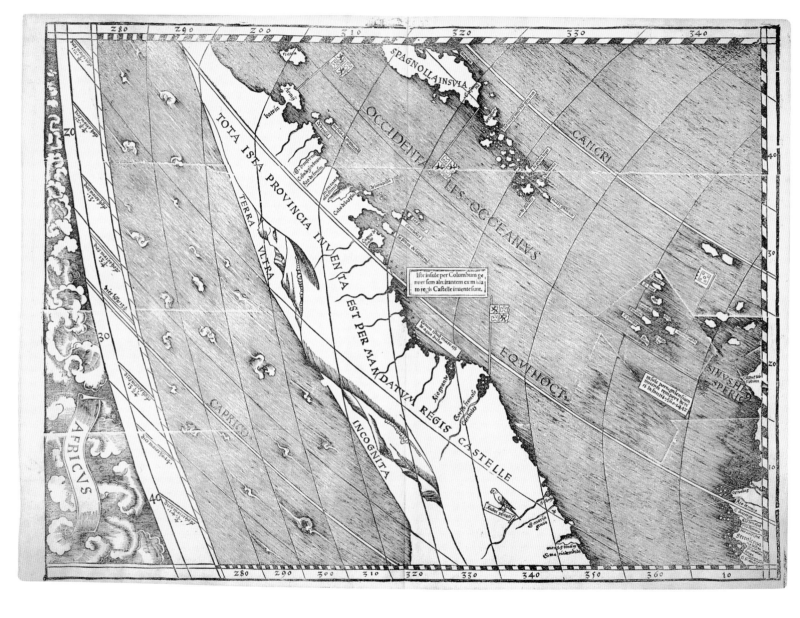

15

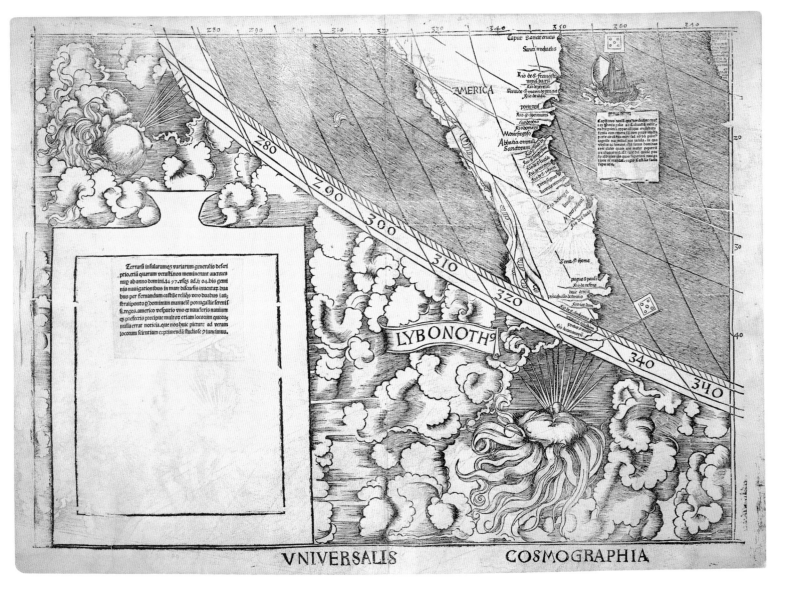

UNIVERSALIS   COSMOGRAPHIA

Sheet 3.

In the middle section of this sheet, the name America is placed on the lower part of what is now South America. Waldseemüller describes this region in the text on the left that reads:

A general delineation of the various lands and islands, including some of which the ancients make no mention, discovered lately between 1497 and 1504 in four voyages over the seas, two commanded by Fernando of Castile, and two by Manuel of Portugal, most serene monarchs, with Amerigo Vespucci as one of the navigators and officers of the fleet; and especially a delineation of many places hitherto unknown. All this we have carefully drawn on the map, to furnish true and precise geographical knowledge.

Sheet 4.

The major portion of this sheet is taken over by a portrait of Ptolemy and an inset map that describes his knowledge of the world.

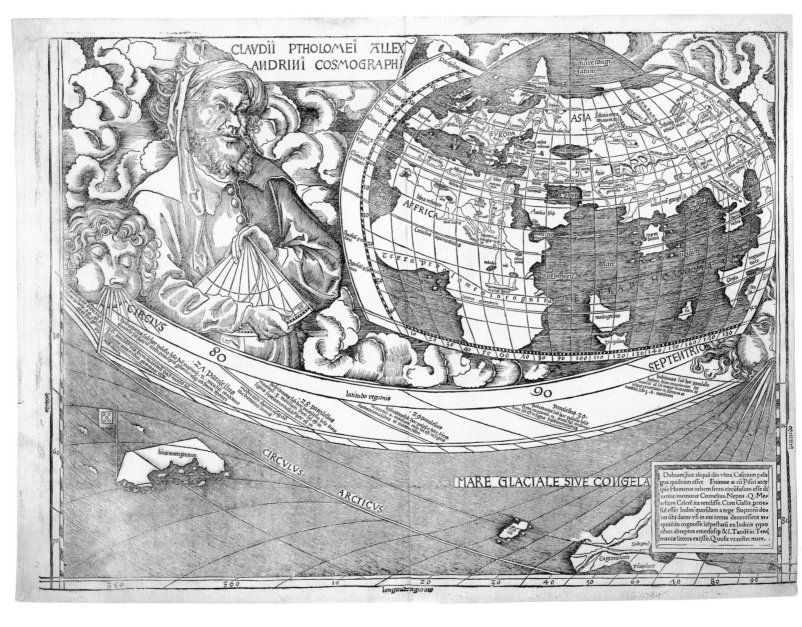

19

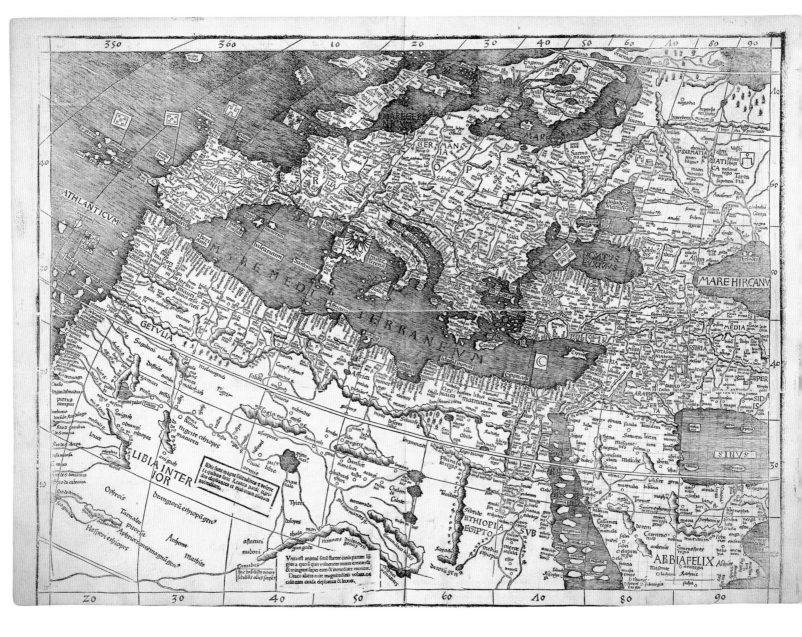

Sheet 5.

The representation of the Mediterranean, Europe and North Africa is
for the most part based on Ptolemy.
On this sheet Schöner drew red lines
over the Middle East north to the
Black Sea region.

Sheet 6.

The lower region of Africa was unknown to Ptolemy and hence Waldseemüller's representation of it is based on newer geographic information. It is interesting that Waldseemüller had to remove a portion of the map's border in order to make room for the lower part of the continent—something he did not do in the case of South America.

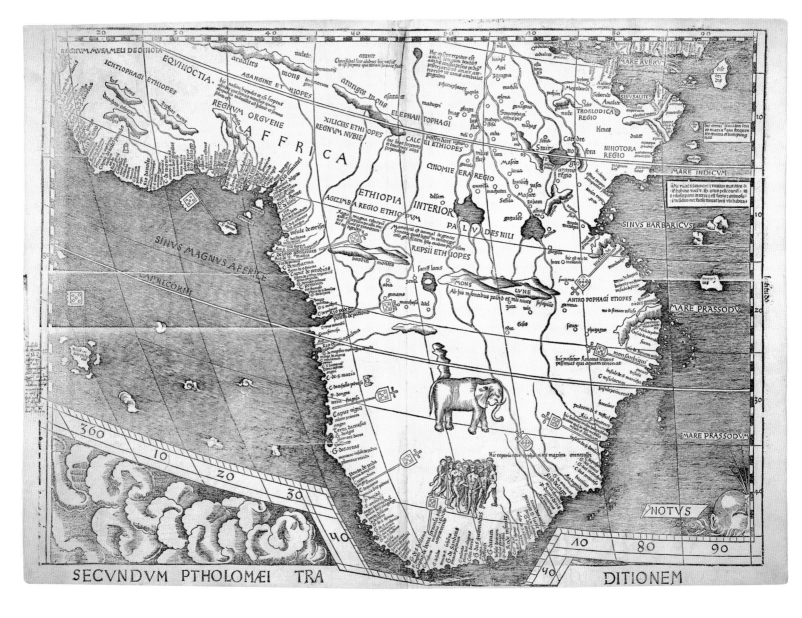

Sheet 7.

The major portion of this sheet is taken up with a portrait of Amerigo Vespucci and an inset map showing his new discoveries. The representation of the New World is slightly different in this inset from that of the entire map in that North and South America remain connected. Another interesting feature is the small wasp that sits off his left shoulder above the word Aquilo.

Sheet 8.

Showing part of the Middle East and South Asia, this sheet contains an area that must have interested Schöner a great deal, as he covered much of the region with a red coordinate grid.

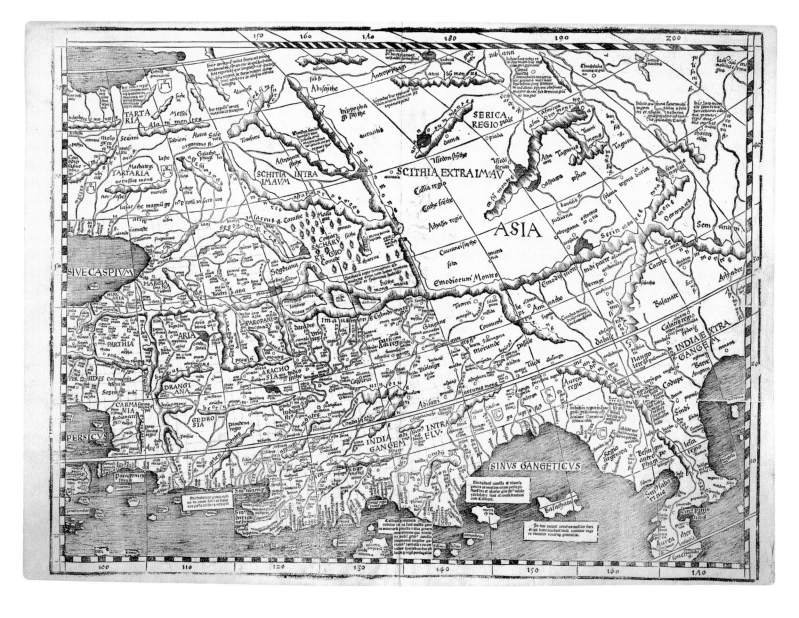

27

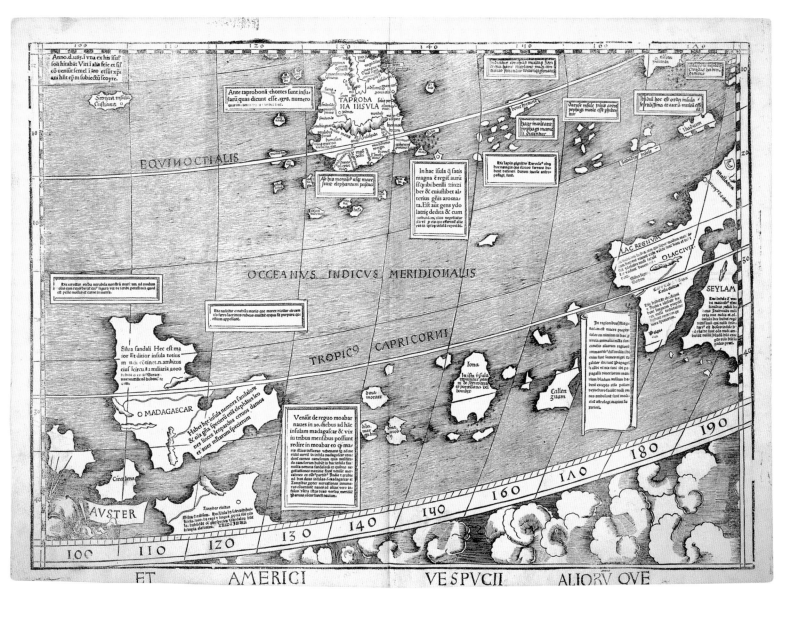

Sheet 9.

This sheet shows the many islands that
Waldseemüller thought existed off
the coast of India, some real and
others fictional.

Sheet 10.

This sheet shows the land of Cathay. Waldseemüller describes this region in the text at the upper right corner, which reads:

In describing the general appearance of the whole world, it has seemed best to put down the discoveries of the ancients, and to add what has since been discovered by the moderns, for instance, the land of Cathay, so that those who are interested in such matters and wish to find out various things may gain their wishes and be grateful to us for our labor, when they see nearly everything that has been discovered here and there, or recently explored, carefully and clearly brought together, so as to be seen at a glance.

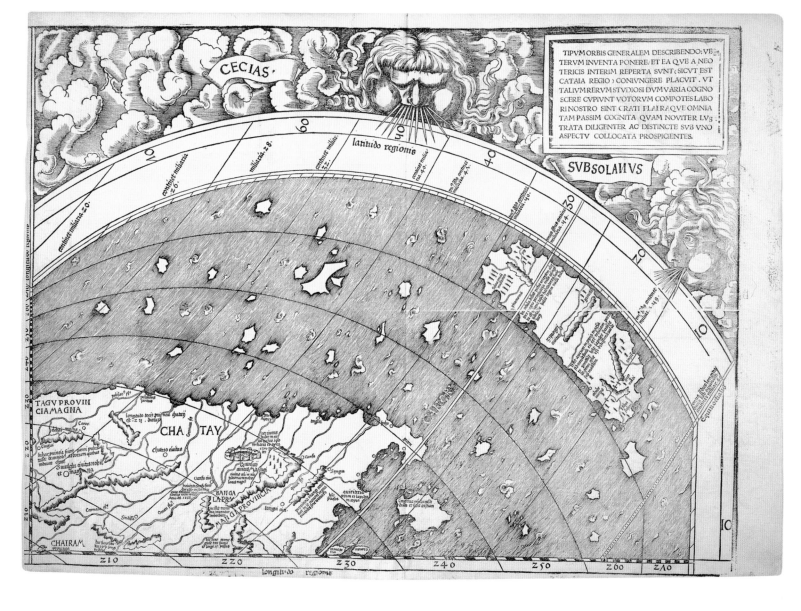

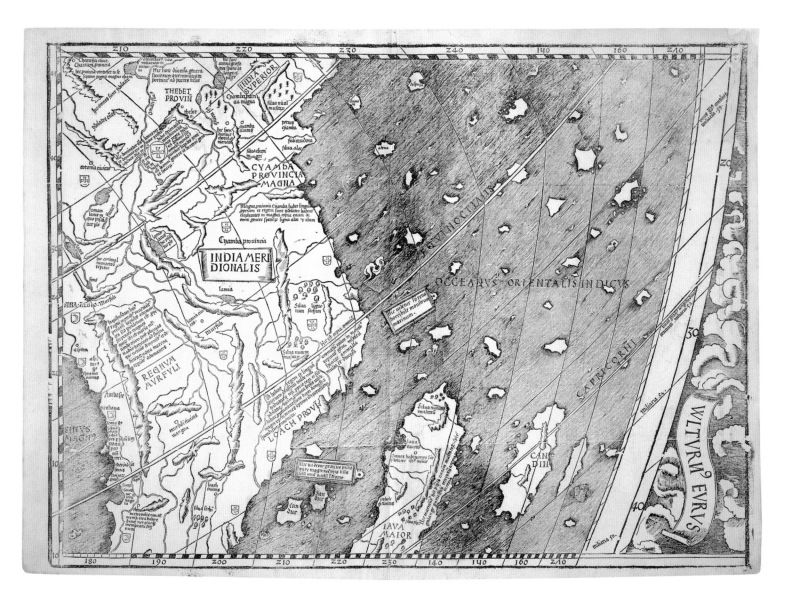

Sheet 11.

This sheet shows the areas supposedly ruled over by Prester John, which Waldseemüller symbolized by placing the cross inside the small shields.

Sheet 12.

In the large text block in the lower right of this sheet, Waldseemüller describes how we are to look at the map. It reads:

Although many of the ancients were interested in marking out the circumference of the world, things remained unknown to them in no slight degree; for instance, in the west, America, named after its discoverer, which is now known to be a fourth part of the world. Another is, to the south, a part of Africa, which begins about seven degrees this side of Capricorn and stretches in a large expanse southward, beyond the torrid zone and the Tropic of Capricorn. A third instance, in the east, is the land of Cathay, and all of southern India beyond 180 degrees of longitude. All these we have added to the earlier known places, so that those who are interested and love things of this sort may see all that is known to us of the present day, and may approve of our painstaking labors. This one request we have to make, that those who are inexperienced and unacquainted with cosmography shall not condemn all this before they have learned what will surely be clearer to them later on, when they have come to understand it.

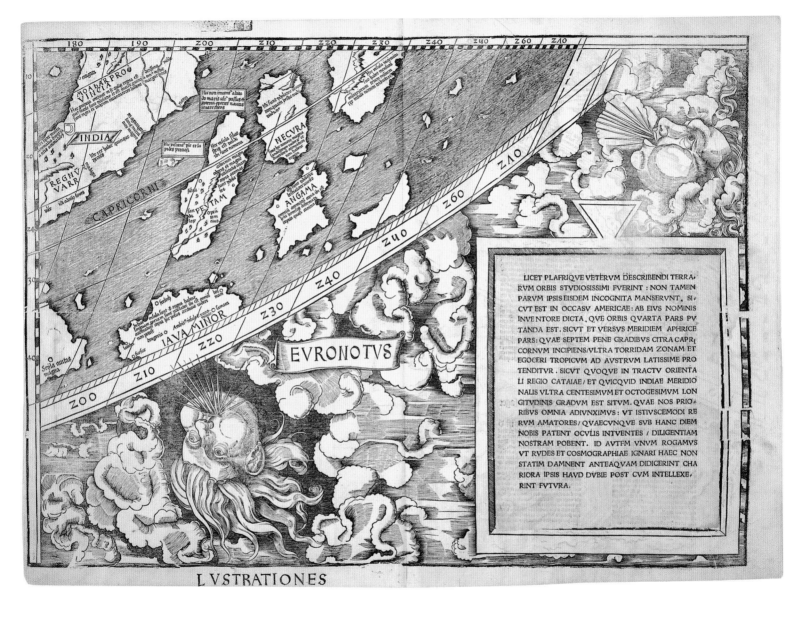

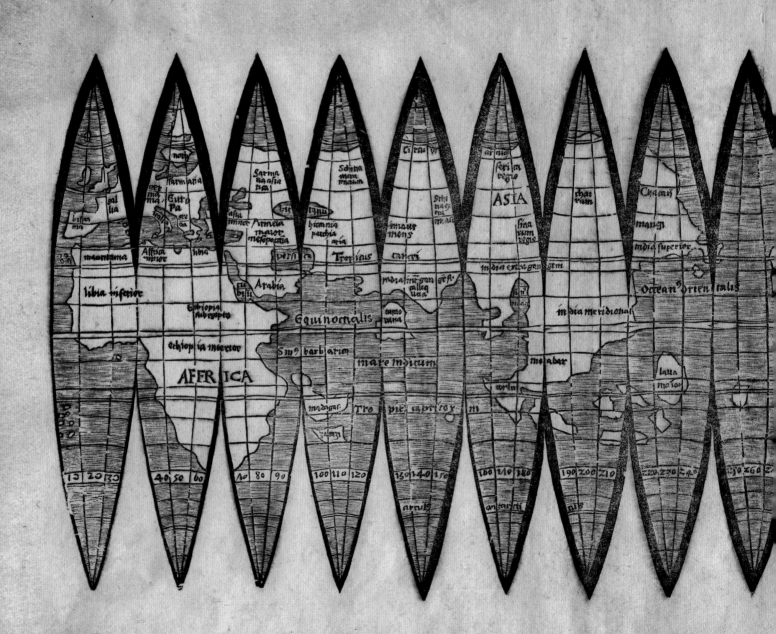

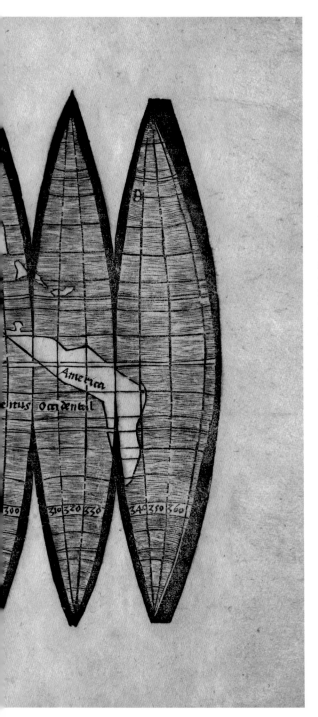

Fig 2.

Globe Gores

The first printed set of globe gores by
Waldseemüller mentioned on the title-
page of the *Cosmographiae Introductio*.
Some controversy exists among scholars
surrounding the date of the printing of
the gores in relation to the 1507 World
Map. Whichever map came first would
be the first map that names America.
We do know that by the summer of 1507
both the map and the gores were available and were purchased by the
Abbott Trithemius in Strasbourg.

Courtesy of the James Ford Bell Library,
University of Minnesota

A New View of the World

An Introduction to Waldseemüller's 1507 World Map
and the *Cosmographiae Introductio*

*What does it mean to obtain a new
concept of the surface of a sphere? How
is it then a concept of the surface of a
sphere? Only in so far as it can be applied
to real spheres.*

Ludwig Wittgentsein [1]

The *Cosmographiae Introductio, cum quibusdam geometriae ac astrono-miae principiis ad eam rem necessariis,* by Martin Waldseemüller (ca. 1470–ca. 1521) and Matthias Ringmann (1482–1511), can be considered one of the most important texts in the history of cartography and per-haps in the history of the Americas as well. Printed in two editions in 1507 in the small town of St. Dié, France, under the patronage of Duke René II of Lorraine, few books of its size have generated as much interest and speculation. The cause for all the attention, both popular and scholarly, stems from the mention on the title-page of two maps that appear to have originally constituted part of the book (figure 1). One of the maps, described in Latin as *in plano* (flat), is Martin Waldsee-müller's famous 1507 World Map, and the other, called *in soliodo* (in the round), was a printed globe gore of his design that is thought to be the first of its kind.

The *Cosmographiae Introductio* and the 1507 World Map by Waldseemüller and Ringmann are transitional documents that occupy an important place in history, coming as they do between the discovery of the New World in 1492 and the birth of the scientific revolution with Copernicus in 1543. They show us a radical representa-tion of the New World and the geography of the Old in a way that today's scholars have yet to fully comprehend. We are not sure how this group of cosmographers from St. Dié utilized their sources, what they had available as evidence, and how they perceived the overthrow of the classical cartography of Ptolemy that their age took to be canonical. Little historical evidence of the circumstances surrounding the creation and printing of the 1507 map survives, but the evidence that we do have, and that we shall discuss here, gives us a window into a time of rapid change when accepted scientific and geographic paradigms fell, spawning the birth of modernity.

For more than three hundred years the only surviving copy of the 1507 map sat unknown and undiscovered in Baden-Württemberg, Germany, on the shelves of the library of the Wolfegg Castle of Prince Waldburg. The map, uncovered there in 1901 by a Jesuit priest, Father Joseph Fischer, was produced by a small group of cosmographers from St. Dié, composed of Gaulthier Ludd (ca. 1448–1527), Mat-thias Ringmann and Martin Waldseemüller. Sometime shortly after 1516 the map was bound into a portfolio known as the Schöner *Sammelbund,* containing the only surviving copy of Waldseemüller's other cartographic masterpiece, the 1516

COSMOGRAPHIAE INTRODVCTIO/ CVM QVIBVSDAM GEOMETRIAE AC ASTRONO MIAE PRINCIPIIS AD EAM REM NECESSARIIS

Infuper quatuor Americi Ve
fpucij nauigationes.

Vniuerfalis Cbofmographiæ defcriptio
tam in folido cpplano/eis etiam
infertis quę Ptholomęo
ignota a nuperis
reperta
funt.

DISTICHON

Cum deus aftra regat/& terræ climata Cæfar
Nec tellus nec eis fydera maius habent.

Fig 1.

Title-Page of the *Cosmographiae Introductio*

This title-page from the first edition of the *Cosmographiae Introductio* by Waldseemüller and Ringmann first announces the famous 1507 World Map and globe gores. The book was published, in at least two editions, in St. Dié, France, by Gaulthier Ludd under the patronage of the Duke of Lorraine.

Courtesy of the Rare Book and Special Collections Division, Library of Congress

world map known as the Carta Marina, by the Nuremberg astronomer, alchemist and globe-maker Johannes Schöner.

How the map arrived in the Castle in Baden-Württemberg, where Fischer discovered it, remains a mystery. It appears that upon Schöner's death in 1545 all of his papers and books passed into the hands of Georg Fugger (d. 1569) and upon his death to his son and great-grandson, Phillip Eduard (1546–1618) and Alfred (1624–82). The Emperor Ferdinand III of Austria purchased Fugger's entire library, containing more than 22,000 books and manuscripts, in 1653 for the Hofbibliothek in Vienna. The circumstances surrounding how and when the portfolio containing the 1507 and 1516 maps became separated from the bulk of Schöner's materials remain, however, unknown. Schöner produced some of the earliest globes that survive from the Renaissance, and the cartographic literature that remains in his collection of books and manuscripts in the National Library of Austria (ONB) reflects his interest in keeping current with the latest level of geographic knowledge. It is therefore no surprise that he should have obtained a copy of the 1507 World Map. The remains of his library are characterized by a great number of handwritten corrections and additions, most of which occur in the margins or on the backs of maps contained in the various editions of Ptolemy that he owned. Schöner was deeply immersed in the study of classical geography and astronomy, and in the dedicatory letter to his edition of Johannes Werner's *Canons* he points out that the study of both of these sciences could not go far without knowledge of the legacy of those who studied the subject before. Schöner calls for their works to be preserved, diligently studied, and expanded upon. He writes that the ancients must be held up as examples, but does not think their work is the final word in these sciences, and that it needs to be improved upon and updated through modern observations. He says, "It is most useful that students of great men become accustomed to the proper practice of these arts [astronomy and cartography] through precepts as well as through examples."[2]

As far as we know Schöner's earliest purchase of a book on the subject of cartography seems to have been a copy of the 1482 Ulm edition of Ptolemy's *Geographia*.[3] A note in Schöner's hand in his copy of that volume explains that he purchased it on 16 October 1507 for about two florins, coincidently just two months after the first known reference to Waldseemüller's map. Bound into Schöner's 1482 Ptolemy are several geographic treatises and lists of coordinates written in his hand that are followed by free-hand drawings of Ptolemy's projections and graphs that try to illustrate the connection between latitude and the length of day, a subject that Waldseemüller will take up in the *Cosmographiae Introductio*. Schöner makes corrections to his Ptolemy in many places and in several different inks, prefiguring the red grid lines that he will draw on his copy of Waldseemüller's 1507 and 1516 maps and that we shall discuss later.

Martin Waldseemüller was born in Freiburg or nearby Wolfenweiler, somewhere around 1475, and died as one of the cathedral canons of St. Dié, probably at the beginning of 1522. The first known authentic information concerning Waldseemüller is found in the matriculation register of the University of Freiburg, where his name is entered on 7 December 1490, as *Martinus Walzenmüller de Friburgo Constantiensis Diocesis*. We unfortunately do not know what course of study he pursued. Matthias Ringmann was born in the Alsace region of France around 1482, possibly studied astronomy and mathematics in Paris with Jacques Lefèvre d'Étaples, and appears to have had an intimate knowledge of ancient Greek. Waldseemüller and Ringmann collaborated on a number of projects that are considered groundbreaking in the history of cartography: the *Cosmographiae Introductio*, the 1507 World Map, the first printed globe gores in 1507, a Ptolemaic atlas printed in 1513 that is extensively corrected using Greek manuscripts and that is the first to explicitly draw a distinction between classical and modern cartography, a large wall map of Europe (now lost) in 1511, and the Carta Marina in 1516.

The exact chronology and dating of all of these works is complicated and not well understood. Waldseemüller and Ringmann worked on several projects simultaneously and because of the death of their patron Duke Rene II in 1508 and the death of Ringmann in 1511 many of the works were completed by others. During the process of creating the 1507 World Map they also worked on the editing of Ptolemy's text and on the maps for their 1513 edition of Ptolemy's *Geographia*. Ringmann collated and compared the previously published texts of the Rome and Ulm editions of the book using a Greek manuscript borrowed from Italy

(Vatican, Cod. Graec. 191).[4] During the early sixteenth century the philological tools for manuscript recension were not yet fully developed so we know little of Ringmann's methods of manuscript comparison.[5] Examining Waldseemüller's correspondence from the period we can see, however, that he and Ringmann were actively seeking rare Greek manuscripts of Ptolemy's *Cosmographia* for their new 1513 edition. In a letter dated the 5 April 1507 he wrote to the Basle bookseller and printer Johannes Amerbach:

> … I think that you are aware that we are going to publish Ptolemy's *Cosmographia* with some new tables revised and added here in the town of St. Dié. And since the exemplars do not agree, I am asking you to oblige me … In the library of the Dominicans near you there is a book of Ptolemy written in Greek letters that I think was thoroughly emended from an authentic version. Therefore I ask you to do whatever must be done in order to borrow that book … for a period of one month.[6]

The maps in the Waldseemüller–Ringmann 1513 edition of Ptolemy include twenty that were prepared based on modern observations. The map of the Upper Rhine Valley that includes the town of St. Dié is particularly interesting in that it was based on the first known systematic field survey. Waldseemüller and Ringmann probably used a *polimetron* with a compass to carry out their measurements and the map that they produced of their home region is accurate to 18 minutes of a degree.[7] The atlas also contains the first printed color map. The project of the new Ptolemy Atlas was put on hold, however, as both Waldseemüller and Ringmann set to work on the 1507 World Map and the *Cosmographiae Introductio*, creations that forever changed the face of the history of cartography and that presented Renaissance Europe with a new view of the world.

The 1507 World Map (figure 2) is arguably one of the most important created in the long history of cartography. The exact circumstances of its creation and the geographic sources used to illustrate its unique vision of the world remain active areas of scholarly research for which few sources or documents survive. Waldseemüller's creation is large and a masterpiece of early woodblock printing.

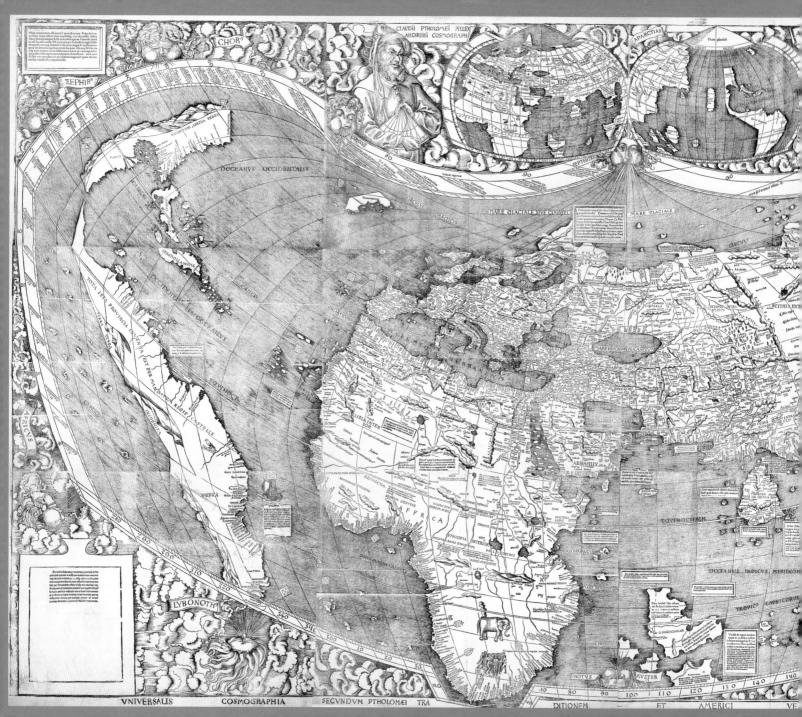

UNIVERSALIS COSMOGRAPHIA SECVNDVM PTHOLOMAEI TRA DITIONEM ET AMERICI VE

Fig 2.

Waldseemüller's 1507 World Map

This composite figure shows the twelve sheets of the 1507 World Map by Martin Waldseemüller and Mathias Ringmann as one large map, approximately 8 feet by 4 feet. Although each of the sheets has borders with latitude and longitude references, they were meant to be displayed as a wall map. This fact probably accounts for the extreme rarity of the map, as few wall maps survived. This copy likely survived because it was found bound into a book.

Produced on twelve individual sheets that when placed together form a single wall map, it shows for the first time the New World separated from Asia and reveals the existence of the Pacific Ocean. According to Waldseemüller's statement on one of the text blocks[8] of the 1516 Carta Marina, the map was printed in 1,000 copies.[9] If this statement is to be believed, the map was certainly too large a project to have been undertaken by the small press at St. Dié. The location of the map's printing is still unknown.[10]

After the printing of the map it appears to have received little attention in cartographic circles even though it presented a radically new understanding of world geography based on the discoveries of Columbus and Vespucci. Waldseemüller himself recognized that the map was an important departure from previous cartographic views of the world and asked for the reader's patience when looking at the map. In the large text block found in the lower right-hand corner of the map we find him saying: "This one request we have to make, that those who are inexperienced and unacquainted with cosmography shall not condemn all this before they have learned what will surely be clearer to them later on, when they have come to understand it." Sadly, his radical new view of the world was noted by few references in contemporary geographic literature and, having been copied by only a few minor cartographers, it slipped into obscurity and disappeared.[11]

Based on their reading of the *Cosmographiae Introductio* in the early and mid-nineteenth century, later scholars, such as Alexander von Humboldt and Marie d'Avezac-Macaya, speculated on the map's existence, on its importance to the early history of the New World, and on its crucial role in the naming of America, all without ever having laid eyes on a copy of the map itself.

The map, which displays the name America for the first time on any map, also represents the continents of North and South America with a shape that is geometrically similar in form to the outlines of the continents as we recognize them today. The two aspects of the shape and the location of the New World on the map, separated as it is from Asia, are chronologically and chronometrically problematic in that in 1507, the map's supposed creation date, neither Vasco Núñez de Balboa nor Ferdinand Magellan had reached the Pacific Ocean.

Fig 3.

Ptolemy's Second Projection

Schematic drawing of Ptolemy's
Second Conic Projection from the
first Greek edition of the *Geographia*
edited by Erasmus of Rotterdam
and published in Basle in 1533.
The text of the *Geographia* has been
widely read in Latin translation by
cartographers and explorers since the
early 16th century and many editions
of the book, both with and without
maps, were printed between 1472 and
Waldseemuller's time. Waldseemuller
and Ringmann themselves produced a
Latin edition of the *Geographia* in 1513.

Courtesy of the Geography and Map Division,
Library of Congress

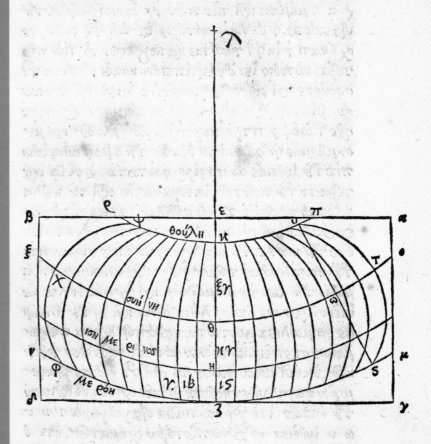

Waldseemüller's representation of the New World has presented a historical and philological enigma for scholars of today. Unanswered questions, such as "How is it possible that a small group of unknown cartographers in the small provincial town of St. Dié could have produced a view of the world so radical for its time and yet so close to the one we recognize today?"; and "Did they have some form of empircal evidence, sailing directions or charts that are unknown today but showed the existence of the Pacific Ocean or was it simply a lucky guess?", abound in the popular and scholarly literature on the map. The cosmographers of St. Dié have not made these questions easy to answer, for they suddenly appear in the historical record around 1505 and then disappear with hardly a trace by 1518. Yet this group of unknowns somehow created three of the most important maps in the history of cartography.

Among the many technical and theoretical problems that Waldseemüller and Ringmann faced in the design and construction of the 1507 map, one of the least trivial was the problem of projection. Map projections are necessary because it is impossible to transform the coordinates and distances on the spherical surface of the earth to those on a flat map without introducing some type of error, whether it be in the shape or the size of landmasses projected. Many ancient cartographers and geographers recognized the difficulties of map projection even before the time of Ptolemy. Dealing with a greatly enlarged earth, due to the discovery of the New World and the charting of the southern half of Africa, the problems of projection reemerged for cartographers in the early sixteenth century. Waldseemüller modified Ptolemy's second projection (figure 3[12]) to account for the New World in a way that unfortunately distorted its shape as it was forced to the far western portion of the map.

In Book I of his *Geographia* Ptolemy laid out instructions on how to construct a world map and a detailed methodology of geometric map projection. The *Geographia* is a technical manual and to understand the text requires a fairly sophisticated knowledge of cartography that Ptolemy assumed on the part of his readers. In chapter 21 of the first book of the *Geographia* Ptolemy says,

> It would be well to keep the lines representing the meridians straight, but to have those that represent the parallels as circular segments described about

one and the same center, from which (imagined as the North Pole) one will have to draw meridian lines.

Ptolemy is trying to achieve a visual effect, a mimetic representation of the earth, rather than something that is simply an accurate map. Again in Book 1, chapter 21, he says, "Above all, the semblance of the spherical surface will be retained." Holding on to Ptolemy's methods of map projection presented problems for Renaissance cartographers trying to show on one map the newly discovered regions of the world that were unknown in classical times.

During Waldseemüller's time, new ideas on map projections were rapidly developing out of the theoretical discussions about Ptolemy's *Geographia*. Many commentators and cartographers realized that there was no reason to adhere to Ptolemy's restriction of a correct representation of distances on only three parallels, a restriction that was introduced in order to construct the circular meridians that preserved a spherical appearance. They found that by altering this arbitrary restriction on the form of the meridians and by applying Ptolemy's methodology to any number of equidistant parallels, they could obtain a map correct on all parallels, with the meridians easily constructible as curves or polygons, connecting points of equal longitude.[13]

In 1514, Johannes Werner produced an important translation and commentary on Book 1 of Ptolemy's *Geographia*. Although this work was printed too late for Waldseemüller to have used Werner's exact methods on the 1507 map, it represents a good summary of the contemporary thinking on map projections. Werner added to his translation a theoretical discussion of two generalizations of Ptolemy's second conic projection in a section of his book entitled *Libellus de quator terrarum orbis in plano figurationibus ab eodem Ioanne Verneo nouissime compertis et enarratis*. In Werner's *Propositio iv* (figure 4) he modified Ptolemy's methodology by requiring that lengths be preserved on all parallels, represented by concentric arcs, and on all radii. He further modified the projection in a way that made the North Pole the center of what in modern language would be called a system of polar coordinates. In *Propositio v*, he also required that a quadrant of the equator have the same length as the radius between a pole and the equator.

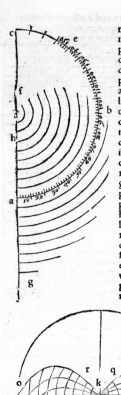

Propofitio.iv.   Planam terrarũ orbis defcriptionẽ conftitue
re:in qua parallelox omnia fegmẽta fimilia: eafdem adinuice obti
nent ratiões:quas paralleli fuper fphæra defcripti. Igĩ fup aliquo
plano:p magnitudinæ & multitudine eox quæ futuræ defcripti
oni funt infcribenda, femicirculus a b c. fup d.centro fcribaĩ: qui
diuiduæ fcindatur fuper b.figno:atɋ vterɋ quadrantũ a b, b c. in
partes feu gradus nonaginta æquales diuidat. Et ipfa a d.in partẽ
a. eiecta pducaĩ vfɋ ad g,fitɋ a g. æqualis ipfi a d. Et vtraɋ duaɋ
linearum a d. & a g,in nonaginta aut in, xviii. æquales partes diui
datur. Per partes itaɋ ipfius a d. & fup d. centro femicirculi quidã
occulti fcribanĩ:q repræfentant parallelos feptentrionales: fimili
modo p diuifiones ipfius a g. rectæ:occultæ quædã circulox cir
cũferentiæ fcribanĩ:quæ fignabũt parallelos meridionales, Hax
itaɋ circũferentiarũ proximæ duæ quæɋ:figurãt proximos du
os fimilis ordinis parallelos: quinis diftãtes gradibʼ:fi vtraɋ ipfa
rum a d. & a g. in decem & octo tantũ partes diuifa fuerit: aut fin
gulis gradibus parallelos diftantes: fi earundẽ a d. & a g. vtraɋ in
partes.xc. fcindaĩ.Earũdẽ itaɋ circũferentiarũ fuprema fit f h.re
præfentãs feptentrionalẽ parallelũ exiftente latitudinis gra.lxxxv.
Et proximus fub eo parallelus erit latitudinis feptentrionalis gra.
lxxx. Et fic deinceps vfɋ ad circulũ a b c. qui æqnoctialis vice ge
ret. In magno tamen affumpto femicirculo a b c. cõueniret diui
dere vtranɋ rectarũ a d.& a g. in nonaginta partes æɋles atɋ de
fcribi p fingulis partibus parallelos. His itaɋ fcriptis parallelis p
eo qui proximus eft d. centro: fi vnius tãtũ gradus diftãtiã a d.
vertice retinet:igitur ex tabula tertiæ ppofitionis: partes. cxli. m̃.
primæ.xx. fumptæ nũerenĩ in circumferentia a b c. & ad exitũ huiʼ
numeratiõis fcribaĩ e. Regulaɋ pofita fup d.vertice atɋ e. figno
cõmunis fectio eiufdem regulæ & circũfe
rentiæ f h. fit f. fignũ:ac ita p fingulis aliis
parallelis fimili modo quædam fiant pun
cta fm oftenfione eiufdem tabule tertiæ p
pofitionis huiʼ.   Rurfus in alio plano re
cta agatur k l m,æqualis ipfi d a g. rectæ li
neæ:bifariam quoɋ diuifa fup l. figno. Et
vtraɋ ipfaɋ k l.l m. in nonaginta æquales
diuidat partes: fiue per fingulas has diuifi
ones fiue per quinas tantũ:æquales tamen
numero & ordine his parallelis fup plano
a b c.fcriptis: etiã fup plano k l m. paralleli
fcribant. fitɋ medius eorũ:qui æqnoctia
lis vice gerit: n l o.circulus. Atɋ definde ex
parallelis plani a b c. fegmenta quæ recta
linea:d a g,atɋ iam factis punctis comphẽ
dunt circini officio transferanĩ : ad æqua
les parallelos plani k l m n o.in vtraɋ par
tem ipfius rectæ k l m. ficut circumferentia
h f.plani a b c d.officio circini transferatur
ad comparem parallelum plani k l m n o.
in vtraɋ parte ipfius k l m.rectæ lineæ:ve
luti fũt p q.p r.circũferẽtiæ plani k l m n o.
quarũ vtraɋ æqualis fit h f. circumferentiæ
plani a b c:atɋ quibufɋ binis pximis pun
ctis p rectas lineas paruulas iugatis: fcribẽ
tur binæ curuæ lineæ quæ fiʼ reddent cor

Fig 4.

Page from Johannes Werner's Commentary on Ptolemy

This is a page from Johannes Werner's important translation and commentary on the first book of Ptolemy's *Geographia*, published in 1514. Werner added innovations to Ptolemy's methods and developed several new map projections that were used by later cartographers. The first book of the *Geographia* contains Ptolemy's theoretical and mathematical treatment of mapmaking and provided the source for several important commentaries on map projections in the early 16th century.

Courtesy of the Geography and Map Division, Library of Congress

These types of modifications were used on Ptolemy's second projection by Waldseemüller to extend his world map to encompass the new discoveries of Vespucci and other European explorers. One major difference between Waldseemüller's world map and that of Ptolemy can be found by looking at the structure of the parallels or lines of latitude. Waldseemüller's parallels are evenly spaced, where Ptolemy's are defined by the length of the longest day at a particular latitude in hour, half-hour and quarter-hour intervals, and are therefore uneven.[14] This is a point that Waldseemüller dwells on extensively in the *Cosmographiae Introductio*.

Waldseemüller and his collaborator Matthias Ringmann discuss the creation and construction of the 1507 map in the *Cosmographiae Introductio*, which was written and printed to be a companion and introduction to the two maps mentioned on the title-page. We do not know whether the 1507 map ever actually accompanied the text of the *Introductio* as Waldseemüller implies, but we do know that both the small globe and the large map were available for sale together. In a letter dated 12 August 1507, the alchemist and cryptographer Johannes Trithemius[15] wrote to his friend Veldicus Monapius that he had "a few days before purchased cheaply a handsome terrestrial globe of small size lately printed at Strasbourg, and at the same time a large map of the world … containing the large islands and countries recently discovered by the Spaniard [sic] Americus Vespucius in the western sea, which extends south almost to the fiftieth parallel."[16]

In the *Cosmographiae Introductio* Waldseemüller describes America by saying, "*Hunc in modum terra iam quadripartita cognoscitur; et sunt tres primae partes continentes / quarta est insula, cum omni quaque mari circumdata conspiciatur* (figure 5).[17] The semantics of his Latin are extremely important here. The passage translates, "The earth is now known to be divided into four parts. The first three parts are continents, but the fourth part is an island, because it has been found to be surrounded on all sides by sea." Waldseemüller uses highly suggestive phrases such as, "now known," and "has been found," both of which imply some form of empirical evidence rather than mere speculation.[18] The question of Waldseemüller's knowledge of the west coast of South America has become the focal point of a great deal of speculation from both a scholarly and a popular perspective.

Capadociam/Pamphiliam/Lidiam/ Ciliciã/ Arme
nias maiorē & minorē. Colchiden/Hircaniam/Hi⸗
beriam/Albaniã:et prꝗterea mlⁱtas quas singilatim
enumerare longa mora esset. Ita dicta ab eius nomi
nis regina.

 Nũc ꝗͦ & hꝗ partes sunt latius lustratæ/& alia
quarta pars per Americũ Vesputiũ(vt in sequenti
bus audietur)inuenta est/quã non video cur quis
iure vetet ab Americo inuentore sagacis ingenīj vi⸗

Ameri⸗
ca
ro Amerigen quasi Americi terrã / siue Americam
dicendã:cũ & Europa & Asia a mulieribus sua sor
tita sint nomina. Eius situ & gentis mores ex bis bi
nis Americi nauigationibus quæ sequunͭ liquide
intelligi datur.

 Hunc in modũ terra iam quadripartita cogno⸗
scit:et sunt tres primꝗ partes cõtinentes/quarta est
insula:cũ omni quaꝗ mari circũdata conspiciaͭ. Et
licet mare vnũ sit quãadmodũ et ipsa tellus/multis
tamen sinibus distincctum/& innumeris replꝗtum

Priscia
nus.
insulis varia sibi noīa assumit:quꝗ et in Cosmogra
phiæ tabulis cõspiciunͭ/& Priscianus in tralatione
Dionisīj talibus enumerat versibus.
Circuit Oceani gurges tamen vndiꝗ vastus
Qui ꝗuis vnus sit plurima nomina sumit.
Finibus Hesperījs Athlanticus ille vocatur
At Boreꝗ qua gens furit Armiaspa sub armis
Diciͭ ille piger necnõ Satur,idē Mortuus est alījs:

Fig 5.

Page [30] from the *Cosmographiae Introductio*

The text on this page describes a "fourth part of the world" discovered by Amerigo Vespucci, and Waldseemüller names it America in his honor. This new part of the globe is said by Waldseemüller to be completely surrounded by water, suggesting that he and Ringmann might have known of the existence of the Pacific Ocean years before its earliest recorded discovery.

Courtesy of the Geography and Map Division, Library of Congress

Theories of unknown Portuguese and Spanish expeditions, the role of Vespucci as the real discoverer of the Straits of Magellan and other more outlandish claims have all been suggested at one time or another even though no real documentary evidence exists to support such ideas.

Within the *Cosmographiae Introductio* Waldseemüller and Ringmann do, however, give us some tantalizing hints about a group of nautical charts that they combined with Ptolemy's geography to produce the 1507 map. They give very little detail in relation to these new sources, saying simply that,

Haec inductione ad Cosmographiae dicta sufficiant si te modo admonuerimus prius, nos in depingendis tabulis typi generalis non omnimodo sequutos esse Ptholomeum, praesertim circa novas terras ubi in cartis marinis aliter animadvertimus equatorium constitui quam Ptholomeus fecerit. Et perinde non debet nos statim culpare qui illud ipsum notaverint. Consulto enim fecimus quod hic Ptholomeum, alibi cartas marinas sequuti sumus.

All that we have said here in our Introduction to Cosmography will provide sufficient understanding only if we tell you that in designing the layout of our world map we have not been faithful to Ptolemy in every respect, particularly in the layout of the new lands, where on the nautical charts we find that the equator has been placed differently than Ptolemy represented it. Therefore when you see this do not think it is our mistake, for we have represented it this way purposely, because at times we have followed Ptolemy and at other times the nautical charts.

What these charts might have been remains a source of great speculation in which, regrettably, no real evidence has emerged. There is no doubt, however, that to create his map Waldseemüller synthesized the best evidence he could find and that he judged to be reliable. On the 1507 map Waldseemüller writes that he and Ringmann, "have carefully drawn all of this on the map, to furnish true and precise geographical knowledge."

On the same page of the *Cosmographiae Introductio* that describes the shape of the new continent Waldseemüller explains why he named it America, and it is certainly the availability of this text, more than the map itself, that led to the persistence and the use of the name by other cartographers, even after Waldseemüller rejected its use on his later maps. The effect of the text can be seen throughout the period and even appears in Copernicus' *De Revolutionibus.* Writing in as late as 1543, Copernicus still ascribes the discovery of America to Vespucci, using a paraphrase of the description of America in the *Cosmographiae Introductio:*

> And, on the other hand in his Cosmography, Ptolemy extended the habitable area halfway around the world. Beyond that point he indicated as unknown land the region where the moderns have placed Cathay and territory as vast as sixty degrees on longitude, so that now the earth is inhabited over a greater stretch of longitude than is left for the ocean. To these regions, moreover, should be added the islands which have been discovered in our time under the Kings of Spain and Portugal, and especially America, named after the ship's captain who discovered it. On account of its as yet undisclosed size it is thought to be a second *orbis terrarum.* There are also many other islands, heretofore unknown. So we have little reason to marvel at the existence of the antipodes or antichthones. For, geometrical consideration of the location of America compels us to believe that it is opposite the Ganges region of India.[19]

Copernicus employs the phrase "alterum orbem terrarum putant," meaning, "they think it to be a second *orbis terrarum,*" and only in this one detail does he vary from Waldseemüller's description. Waldseemüller conceived of America as the fourth part of the world because he viewed Asia, Europe, and Africa as separate continents. Copernicus defines these three as the first *orbis terrarum* and as a single large continent and therefore places America in a new second *orbis terrarum.*

Another important historical question that has yet to be properly answered by scholars stems from the use of the 1507 map by its owner, Johannes Schöner. In 1515 Schöner produced a globe that, unlike Waldseemüller's map, clearly shows a passage around the coast of South America and into the Pacific Ocean before any was known. The globe, of which only two copies survive, may have been based on Waldseemüller's map and also on sources that are no longer extant but that Waldseemüller may also have had access to. Because Johann Schöner's 1515 globe depicts a passage around South America, many scholars have been led to speculate that Schöner used Waldseemüller's 1507 map as a model, hypothesizing that the red grid lines drawn by him on the map (see figure 6) were used to rescale the map to the size of the globe gores. In Schöner's extant library there is a notebook of geographical information that forms a miscellany containing various notes on coordinates and technical information on maps.[20] In one section of the notebook, entitled the *Regionum Distantiae*, Schöner discusses methods for projecting flat maps onto globes, describing a gridding technique that he may have himself used in the creation of his globes.[21]

Although Waldseemüller's 1507 map does not explicitly show a passage around South America, it does depict the continent detached from Asia, suggesting the passage exists. Elizabeth Harris, in her study of the typography on the 1507 map, concluded, basing her argument on the condition of the woodblocks and other physical evidence from the watermarks and the fonts used, that the copy of the map that Schöner owned could not have been printed before 1515.[22] If Harris' date is correct then Schöner's use of Waldseemüller's map as a model would not be a possible explanation for his first depiction of the passage. Harris' work is compelling and there are few scholars working in the field today who argue with her conclusions. But Schöner's drawing of the grid on the 1507 map and others in his library[23] leads one to believe that he actively analyzed and used the 1507 map, perhaps as a source for a later globe or to correct longitudes for the use in the casting of horoscopes.

One likely source for both Waldseemüller and Schöner's description of the passage under South America is a rare German pamphlet, *Copia der Newen Zeytung aus Pressillg Landt,*[24] according to which a Portuguese expedition of two vessels had tried to sail through the passage from the east, but was forced back by winds.[25] Ritter von Wieser[26] supposes that the expedition had to have taken place in the late fifteenth or early sixteenth century (before 1509), making the pamphlet a possible source for both Schöner and Waldseemüller if it was composed before 1507.

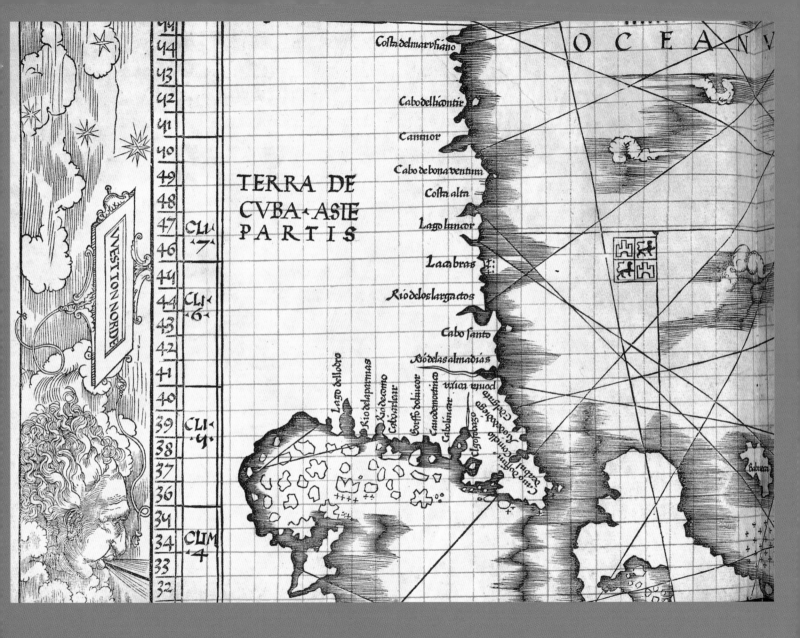

Fig 6.

**Schöner's red lines on the 1516
Carta Marina**

The Nuremburg astronomer and
globe maker Johannes Schöner drew
red lines such as these on sections
of Waldseemüller's 1507 world map
(see sheets 5 and 8, pp. 20 and 27
above). This figure shows the grid
of lines that Schöner drew on the
1516 Carta Marina for the purpose of
determining the coordinates of various locations to be used either for his
globes or the casting of horoscopes.
Schöner bound the 1516 and 1507
maps together sometime after 1516
into a book that has become known
as the Schöner *Sammelbund*.

Courtesy of the J. Kislak Collection, Rare Book
and Special Collections Division, Library of
Congress

That Schöner used the *Newen Zeytung* as a source is strongly indicated by the description of the lands of "Brazil" in his *Luculentissima quaedam terrae totius descriptio,* which was written as a guide to his globe much in the way the *Cosmographiae Introductio* was written for the 1507 map. Schöner's book discusses the people, animals and customs in the same way and using much the same language as the *Newen Zeytung* and also gives a description of the two parts of the New World and its location as it is shown on Waldseemüller's 1507 World Map. The *Newen Zeytung* is a small and extremely rare pamphlet of only four pages. The work is known in two different editions, one bearing a woodcut of a Portuguese coat of arms and the other with a woodcut showing islands and ships. This pamphlet, like the *Cosmographiae Introductio,* was much discussed in the nineteenth century and both Alexander von Humboldt and Marie Armand d'Avezac-Macaya commented on it.[27] Serious consideration of the text begins with von Weiser who, through philological and linguistic evidence, presented the view that the original text was in German and that the expedition that it describes could not have taken place after 1509, reaching as far south as St. Matias Bay.[28]

In what is perhaps the most extensive commentary on the book, Rodolpho Schuller disagrees with von Weiser's analysis of the linguistic evidence.[29] Schuller finds that in the four pages of text there are some forty words of Portuguese, Spanish and Italian origin and that this is in fact a German translation of an earlier text or based on another work.

The narrative is quite similar to both Vespucci's *Four Voyages* and the *Mundus Novus* with a critical difference being that the text does describe a ship rounding the continent:

> When we came to the Cape … which is a point jutting out into the ocean at the level of Nort Assril and perhaps one degree higher or further in latitude … And they sailed around this very cape and found that the same gulf lies as Europe does, with the side lying *ponente levante*, that is, situated between sunrise or east and sunset or west. Then they saw land on the other side as well when they had sailed a distance of sixty miles along the cape in the same manner as when one travels toward the east and passes the *Stritta Gibilterra* and sees the

land of the Berbers. And when they came around the cape as stated and sailed or traveled northwestward toward us, there arose such a great storm and also such wind that they were unable to sail or travel further. Hence they had to sail through *tramontana*, that is northward or midnight, and back again to the other side and coast that is the land of Brazil.[30]

The location of Nort Assril in the above quote remains unknown but the text clearly describes a passage around South America that resembles the straits of Gibraltar. According to Schuller the *Newen Zeytung* must derive from the writings of Vespucci that have been supplemented by unknown Portuguese sources.

The *Cosmographiae Introductio* is divided into two distinct parts. The first, and the section translated here, consists of various chapters that serve as Waldseemüller and Ringmann's introduction to cosmography and to the technical definitions necessary for the reader and observer to understand the accompanying maps. The second part contains Johannes Basinus Sendacurius' Latin translation of an unknown French edition of the *Quatuor Americi Vespucii navigationes* (*The Four Voyages of Amerigo Vespucci*). [31]

The history of the transmission of Vespucci's discoveries is directly tied to the researches of the group at St. Dié and to the *Cosmographiae Introductio*. Gaultius Ludd, the canon at St. Dié under whose guidance the press that published the *Introductio* operated, writes in the dedication of his small book from 1507, the *Speculi orbis succincta sed neque poenitenda neque inelegans declaratio et canon,*[32] to René II, Duke of Lorraine and King of Jerusalem, "But we would not deny that, in place of the enlarged delineation of Europe here given, might properly be inserted the representation which we have hastily prepared of the unknown land discovered some time since by the King of Portugal." Ludd goes on to refer to "a description of those regions in French sent to you from Portugal, most illustrious King René" and "translated into Latin at my instance by the notable poet Johannes Basinus Sendacurius," and to a certain epigram of Philesius Vogesigena (Ringmann) printed in the tract translated from Italian into Latin. Ludd is referring to two distinct versions of Vespucci's letters and narratives. The first is the so-called "Letter to Soderini" describing the four voyages of which Basinus made a Latin translation of a French copy, this becoming the text included in the *Cosmographiae Introductio*. The other is the edition of the *Mundus*

Novus that had been prepared by Ringmann and printed in Strasbourg in 1505 under the title *De Ora Antarctica per Regem Portugalliae pridem Inventa.*

The version of the Soderini Letter used by Waldseemüller and Ringmann is thought to exist as an independent branch of the recension of the text and therefore closer to the lost original version than other forms of the Letter.[33] A recension can be thought of as a kind of linguistic genealogy. During copying and editing, manuscripts and printed materials have mistakes, deletions, and additions made to them, which are then recopied and continued through the history of the text as later copies and printings are made. By looking closely at these and other linguistic evidence, such as place-names and words borrowed from other languages, it is sometimes possible to reconstruct how the text was transmitted through its history and to identify independent versions.

Besides the version of the Soderini Letter used by Basinus and Waldseemüller, there are two other versions of the text that exist and have become known as the Florentine Print and the Magliabechiana Manuscript, both of which are in Italian. The linguistic relationship of Basinus' text to these other known forms remains problematic. In the *Cosmographiae Introductio,* Waldseemüller sheds some light on the problem by mentioning that the text of Vespucci translated into Latin by Basinus comes from a French translation of an Italian original.

In 1907 Joseph Fischer[34] and Franz von Wieser translated the *Cosmographiae Introductio* into English in an edition that suffers from a number of drawbacks. First, Fischer's translation is archaic in its style and does not always accurately reflect the Latin prose employed by Waldseemüller, Ringmann and Basinus. Second, and more importantly, the translation appears without any critical apparatus or commentary that would help the modern reader understand the context of the book and the unanswered historical questions that surround the 1507 World Map that it accompanied. The current edition seeks to provide a modern translation of the text and a critical commentary that has benefited from over a century of new scholarship on the *Introductio,* on the 1507 map and on the text of Vespucci's voyages. The commentary, in the form of detailed translator's notes, identifies the sources of quotes, the persons mentioned by Waldseemüller and Ringmann, and explains many of the concepts that the authors took for granted that their readers would know. These notes not only help the modern reader understand Waldseemüller's text, but also provide an important introduction to the current debates surrounding the 1507 World Map and his later cartographic works.

The text of the *Cosmographiae Introductio* resembles, in its technical descriptions of what Waldseemüller and Ringmann term "necessary cosmographical principles," what was perhaps the most widely read astronomy textbook of the period, the *Tractatus de Sphaera (Sphere)* of Johannes Sacrobosco (1195–1236).[35] In 1495 there appeared in Paris an important commentary on the *Sphere* authored by Matthias Ringmann's teacher Jacques Lefèvre d'Étaples (ca. 1455–1536),[36] and both Waldseemüller and Ringmann would certainly have been very familiar with it. The *Sphere* is written in a much clearer and straightforward fashion than the *Cosmographiae Introductio* but shares a common subject matter and form of presentation. There are several places in Waldseemüller's text where he uses the same language as the *Sphere* and employs the same quotes from classical authors. For example, in chapter 2 of the *Introductio*, where Waldseemüller is describing the axis of the poles, he uses the same Virgil quote at the end of his explanation. The *Sphere* begins its description,

> It is to be noted that the pole which always is visible to us is called "septentrional," "arctic," or "boreal." "Septentrional" is from *septentrio*, that is, from Ursa Minor, which is derived from *septem* and *trion*, meaning "ox," because the seven stars in Ursa move slowly, since they are near the pole. Those seven stars are also called *septentriones* as if *septem teriones*, because they tread the parts about the pole. "Arctic" is derived from *arthos*, which is Ursa Major, for it is near Ursa Major. It is called "boreal" because it is where the wind Boreas comes from. The opposite pole is called "Antarctic" as opposed to "Arctic." It also is called "meridional" because it is to the south, and it is called "austral" because it is where the wind Auster comes from. The two fixed points in the firmament are called the "poles of the world" because they terminate the axis of the sphere and the world revolves on them. One of these poles is always visible to us, the other always hidden. Whence Virgil: 'One pole is ever high above us while the other, beneath our feet, is seen of black Styx and shades infernal.'

In order to explain the same concept Waldseemüller's text begins,

> The poles, which are called the *cardines*, and the vertices terminate the axis of the sphere and are points that never move. Our explanation of the axis and poles of the material sphere are referred to the eighth sphere because it resembles it as a limited version. On the material sphere there are two principal poles, one the northern, also called Arcticus and Borealis, the other the southern, called Antarcticus. Hence Virgil says: "One pole is ever high above us while the other, beneath our feet, is seen of black Styx and shades infernal."[37]

There are many other parallels in both of the texts that I point out in the annotations to the translation.

In many places in the *Cosmographiae Introductio* Waldseemüller quotes from or mentions various geographers, philosophers and poets. To the best of my ability I have tried to identify the sources of the quotes and the editions of the texts that Waldseemüller may have used. Most of the quotes are from Greek and Roman geographers and not from contemporary sources. Two interesting examples come from Waldseemüller's use of Pomponius Mela and Dionysius Periegetes. Waldseemüller quotes from Pomponius Mela's *Cosmographia, sive De Situ Orbis*,[38] one of the few geographical texts from the early Roman Empire that have survived. The *De Situ Orbis* is written in three books and contains a description of a portion of world geography. Mela's layout of the continents is divided into two hemispheres surrounded by water and divided into five climatic zones from north to south as is found in any number of classical sources such as Eratosthenes' poem *Hermes* or Virgil's *Georgics*. Waldseemüller uses Mela in a portion of the *Introductio* discussing Vespucci's new discoveries that describes a land to the south that is separated from us by an uninhabitable zone of great heat and is therefore unknown to Europeans.

Mela's description comes out of a long tradition of Greek chorography. *Chorographia* in Latin typically designates a written description of some limited portion of the world. This can be contrasted with other categories of geographical writing that survived from the classical period and into the Renaissance such as *topographia*, writing about a single place; *geographia,* writing about the whole world; and *cosmographia,* writing about the whole universe. Mela knew that he could not hope to describe the entire inhabited world and this recognition is brought out in his theory of the counter-world, or antichthone, that is symmetrical on the earth with the part we inhabit: "The habitable zones have the same season, but not at the same time. The antichthones inhabit one, and we the other. The situation of the former zone is unknown because of the heat of the intervening expanse." Waldseemüller employs Mela's words to aid in his explanation of our lack of knowledge of the new southern lands of the sixth climate toward Antarctica, a region he believes to have been recently discovered by Amerigo Vespucci.

One of the strangest geographical texts that Waldseemüller utilized was Priscian's translation of Dionysius Periegetes. The quotes that he takes from Dionysius take up nearly five pages in the *Cosmographiae Introductio* and we cannot be certain why he chose to rely on such a minor Greek geographer. Dionysius, who was a contemporary of Ptolemy, in his *Descriptive Account of the Habitable World* (AD 124), [39] seeks to give an account in verse of the entire world as it was known in the second century. This account is a poem of about 1,200 lines, written, according to Dionysius, not to provide some new geographical knowledge but rather to enlarge the minds of his readers. The text is therefore a summary of well-known descriptions of oceans, countries, and islands with important details that a cultivated reader of the Hadrianic period of Rome needed to know. His description of the world differs from that of any other ancient writer in that he describes the continents of Europe and of Africa as forming a great cone, the base of which defines the line separating them both from Asia. Dionysius tells us up front that he did not arrive at his knowledge of geography through traveling in the hulls of ships to distant lands but rather through the reading of books. Waldseemüller may have felt a kinship with Dionysius as he expresses a similar sentiment in the very beginning of the *Introductio,* "few will deny that it is also profitable to learn from books the locations of lands, cities and the customs of foreign peoples." It is important in approaching both his map and his text that we recall that Waldseemüller's vision of the world was that of a scholar and humanist and not that of a sailor or navigator.

The style of Waldseemüller and Ringmann's Latin prose and poetry found in the *Cosmographiae Introductio* is typical of many early texts on astronomy and cartography in that it appears choppy and fragmented to the modern reader.

There seems to be a poverty of words and explanations and there is in the text a certain lack of narrative flow that on first reading may strike one as simplistic. We must remember when we approach the text of the *Introductio* that it is meant to be a guidebook to the 1507 World Map and that Waldseemüller and Ringmann, like Ptolemy before them, assumed a certain familiarity on the part of the reader with classical notions of astronomy and geography, and the conventions of fifteenth-century writing on these subjects.

In the end, the world maps of Waldseemüller and Ringmann are perfect philological objects for the historian of cartography and as such display in stark relief the dual paradox that is at the heart of all cartography. On the one hand, there is the map's symbolic power; its mythic and semantic meanings which come to the fore whenever a viewer's eyes pass over it. In this sense the Waldseemüller maps constitute a space where cultural memories are invoked, a view of a world newly discovered that is at once strange but also somehow familiar and comforting in its comprehensibility to the modern viewer. On the other hand, there is this object of pure rationality, an intellectual space born of the science of the early sixteenth century. This is the space of the mapmaker and is dominated by geometry, geographical knowledge, and symmetry all combined in an empirical order to make a model of the world to be read and understood as true. What we must realize is that these two aspects of the map are in reality two different and incommensurate forms of logic and understanding, one for the modern spectator and one for the author. As modern spectators we are free to theorize, to speculate and to attempt to understand, but we must also accept that we shall never cross the profound intellectual gulf that stands between us and Waldseemüller's conception of his world. As the mathematical astronomer Alex Clairaut said in the eighteenth century, "there is a great distance between a truth that is glimpsed and one that is proved."[40] New research by scholars may reveal more facts, but we shall never truly grasp the cartographic gesture of Waldseemüller and Ringmann, a gesture that came at a time when it was still possible to construct a new view of the world.

Notes and References

1 Ludwig Wittgenstein, *Remarks on the Foundations of Mathematics*, ed. G.H. von Wright and translated by G.E.M. Anscombe (Cambridge: MIT Press, 1983), 259.

2 Johannes Werner, *Canones sicut brevissimi, ita etiam doctissimi, complectentes praecepta et observationes de mutatione aurae,* (Nuremberg: Joannes Montanus and Ulrichus Neuber, 1546), folios A2^{r/v}.

3 The following items from Schöner's books in the National Library of Austria are important to the study of the Waldseemüller maps:

I. **1482 Ulm edition of Ptolemy**
ONB, Handschriftensammlung, Codex 3292
Purchased by Schöner on 16 October 1507
Contains manuscripts in Schöner's hand:
1. *De locis ac mirabilibus mundi et primo de tribus orbis partibus*
2. *Registrum super tractatum de tribus orbis partibus*
3. *Registratum alphabeticum super octo libros Ptolemei*
4. *De mutatione nominorum*
This volume also contains two manuscript drawings of the first two Ptolemaic projections and a diagram *Lineares demonstrationes Parallelorum Ptholemei.*

II. **Cosmographiae Introductio** by Waldseemüller and Ringmann
First edition, April 1507
ONB, CPi D 53
Schöner's copy is annotated throughout in his hand.

III. **1513 Strasbourg Ptolemy**
ONB, Kartensammlung, 393.692 D.K.
Volume contains a hand-colored world map that differs in several aspects from the usual map found in the 1513 atlas in that it has a primitive printed grid superimposed over the map. Both the classical and modern maps also have red grid lines that resemble those found on the 1507 and 1516 World Maps. Many of the modern maps are annotated with circles around place names.

IV. **1509 "Deutsch Ptolemy"**
ONB, Handschriftensammlung, Codex 2992
This is a small booklet that contains in Schöner's hand a summary of books 1 and 7 taken from the so-called German Ptolemy of 1490. Notes also contain information that resembles the *Cosmographiae Introductio.*

V. **Geographical notebooks**
ONB, Handschriftensammlung, Codex 3505
Contain instructions on globe construction, distance measurement techniques and a large group of coordinate lists.

4 This codex is on paper and contains a large corpus of mathematical and scientific writings copied by many hands. The text of the *Geography* is for the most part in three hands except in the beginning where some missing pages have been replaced by pages in a fourth. This manuscript or something derived from it is thought to have been used by Ringmann because it is the only known extant copy that is free from the Byzantine corrections, a few of which also do not appear in the 1513 coordinate lists. This is of course a highly speculative attribution.

5 The classic study of the development of scholarly methods of manuscript comparison and criticism can be found in Anthony Grafton's book, *Joseph Scaliger: A Study in the History of Classical Scholarship* (Oxford: Oxford University Press, 1983).

6 Johann Amerbach, *The Correspondence of Johann Amerbach: Early Printing in its Social Context*, trans. Barbara C. Halporn (Ann Arbor: University of Michigan Press, 2000). Amerbach was one of the most important printers and booksellers in Basle during the early part of the 16th century. His correspondence is part of a collection of letters of the Amerbach family held by the Universitätsbibliothek at the University of Basle. The letters from the collection were edited by Alfred Hartmann in the 10-volume series *Die Amerbachkorrespondenz,* beginning in 1942.

7 E.G.R. Taylor, "Cartography, Survey and Navigation, 1400–1750," in *A History of Technology* (Oxford: Oxford University Press, 1957), 530–37.

8 Text from the lower right-hand sheet of the Carta Marina says, *"Generalem igitur totius orbis typum, quem ante annos paucos absolutum non sine grandi labore ex Ptolemei traditione, auctore profecto prae nimia vetustate vix nostris temporibus cognito, in lucem edideramus et in mille exemplaria exprimi curavimus."*

9 Typical press runs for books of the period

were between 800 and 1,000 copies. The numbers for maps, however, have proved elusive. For more on publishing in Alsace and northern France see Miriam Chrisman, *Lay Culture, Learned Culture: Books and Social Change in Strassburg 1480–1599*, (New Haven: Yale University Press, 1982).

10 Most scholars believe that the 1507 world map was printed in Strasbourg either by Johannes Gruninger or by Johannes Schott.

11 One of those cartographers was Heinrich Glarean or Loritti (Glareanus), who inserted into his copy of the 1482 Ulm Ptolemy a manuscript map dated 1510 that resembles that of Waldseemüller and says that he followed the "Deodatensian or preferably the Vosgien geographer."

12 Figure taken from the first printed Greek edition of Ptolemy. The edition was edited by Erasmus and printed in Basle in 1533. *Klaudiou Ptolemaiou Alexandreos philosophou en tois malista pepaideumenou, peri tes geographias biblia okto, meta pases akribeias entypothenta, Claudii Ptolemaei Alexandrini philosophi cum primis eruditi, De geographia libri octo, summa cum uigilantia excusi* (Basle: H. Frobenius and N. Episcopius), 1533.

13 Claudius Ptolemy, *Ptolemy's Geography: An Annotated Translation of the Theoretical Chapters*, trans. J. Leurant Bergsen and Alexander Jones (Princeton: Princeton University Press, 2000).

14 Aubrey Diller, "The Parallels on Ptolemaic Maps," *Isis* 33 (1941), 4–7.

15 Johannes Trithemius was the Abbot of Sponheim and an associate of many of the Alsacian humanists in the circle of those from St. Dié such as the printers and booksellers Johannes Amerbach and Johann Heynlin. His early work, *De Ecclesiasticis Scriptoribus,* was published by Amerbach in 1494 and is a bio-bibliography of pro-Catholic writings. He left the abbey in 1506. Trithemius was also an astrologer and cryptographer. His most important work in this realm is called the *Steganographia*. At first reading the book appears to be a system of magic, but in reality it is meant to be a highly sophisticated system of cryptography. It claims to contain a synthesis of the science of knowledge and therefore logic, the art of memory, magic, an accelerated language learning system, and a method of sending messages without symbols or a messenger. The manuscript circulated extensively but Trithemius decided it should never be published. For more see Noel Brann, *The Abbot Trithemius (1462–1516): The Renaissance of Monastic Humanism* (Leiden: E.J. Brill, 1981).

16 Johannes Trithemius, *Epistularum Familarium* (Hagehau, 1536), 296.

17 [Martin Waldseemüller and Mathias Ringmann], *Cosmographiae Introductio* (St. Dié, 1507), p. [30].

18 The possibility of empirical evidence for Waldseemüller's portrayal of the New World has recently been studied using polynomial warping computer models. See John Hessler, "Warping Waldseemüller: A Phenomenological and Computational Study of the 1507 World Map," *Cartographica* 41 (2006), 101–13.

19 Nicholas Copernicus, *De Revolutionibus Orbium Caelestium* (Nuremburg, 1543), book 1, ch. 3. English translation by Edward Rosen, *On the Revolutions* (Baltimore: Johns Hopkins University Press, 1978).

20 ONB, Handschriftensammlung, Codex 3505.

21 The most interesting of all these works in Schöner's notebook is the *Regionum sive Civitatum*. The treatise begins by describing a set of instructions for constructing a terrestrial globe. The initial part of the text describes the process by which one inscribes on a globe the locations of the cities and regions on the earth. The first set of instructions divides the earth into four equal areas by means of two arcs that intersect each other at 90-degree angles. Once these circles have been inscribed on the globe another great circle is drawn that bisects the other two and forms the equator. The next step divides that part of the equator that lies along the "habitable" part of the earth into 180 degrees of longitude, numbering them in units of five. For marking the globe with latitude lines a strip of heavy vellum is used, equal in length to the distance from the pole to the equator. This type of construction continues in the various regions until the whole surface of the globe has coordinates. In order to transpose the points and locations of cities and regions from the globe to a plane the method is essentially that of an azimuthal projection from any point on the surface of the earth. At first the globe-maker selects the city or point that he wishes to make the center of the projected map. Then with a compass he inscribes a

circle on the surface of the globe that is large enough in diameter to include the area to be reproduced. The smaller the circle, the larger the scale of the resulting map and the greater ease involved in measuring distances. The second method described in the book outlines what appears to be a conic projection. To do this, two new vellum strips are used, equal in length to the diameter of the circle drawn on the surface of the globe. The strips are divided into the same number of degrees as the strips used in the first method. They are then placed tangentially along the circle, running north to south. The text says that this method can be used either on a square (*quadratam*) or a circular (*rotundam*) map. All this suggests that Schöner was experimenting a great deal with different methods for measuring distances and for transferring coordinates from maps to globes and vice versa and obviously drew his annotations on the 1507 and 1516 World maps by Waldseemüller for this purpose.

22 Elizabeth Harris, "The Waldseemüller World Map: A Typographic Appraisal," *Imago Mundi* 37 (1985), 30–53.

23 Schöner drew red grid lines on a number of maps in his library including his copy of the 1513 Strasbourg Ptolemy. Schöner's notebooks and coordinate list have yet to be properly studied in the context of the 1507 and 1516 maps of Waldseemüller.

24 The pamphlet is reproduced and translated with commentary in M. Graubard and J. Parker, *Copia der Newen Zeytung aus Pressillg Landt, Tidings out of Brazil* (Minneapolis, 1957).

25 Chet Van Duzer, "The Cartography, Geography and Hydrography of the Southern Ring Continent, 1515–1763," *Orbis Terrarum* 8 (2002), 115–58.

26 F. Ritter von Wieser, *Magalâes-Strasse und Austral-Continent. Auf den Globen des Johannes Schöner* (Innsbruck, 1881).

27 Alexander von Humboldt, *Examen critique de l'histoire de la géographie du nouveau continent*, vol. 5 (Paris: Librarie de Gide, 1859). Marie Armand d'Avezac-Macaya, "Considerations géographiques sur l'histoire du Brésil," *Bulletin de la Société Géographique*, 4th series 14 (1857), 90–356.

28 Von Wieser (1881).

29 Rudolpho Schuller, ed., *A nova gazeta da terra do Brasil* (Rio de Janeiro, 1914).

30 *Newen Zeytung*, 28–29.

31 A critical edition and excellent translation of the text of the *Four Voyages* was published in 1916 by George Tyler Northrup under the title *Amerigo Vespucci: Letter to Piero Soderini*. This remains the best scholarly translation and would be difficult to improve upon.

32 Published in 1507 in Strasbourg by Johannes Gruninger.

33 Amerigo Vespucci, *Letter to Piero Soderini*, edited and translated by George Tyler Northup (Princeton: Princeton University Press, 1916), 16.

34 [Martin Waldseemüller and Mathias Ringmann], *Cosmographiae Introductio* (St. Dié, 1507). Reprinted by Joseph Fischer and Franz von Wieser, *The Cosmographiae Introductio of Martin Waldseemüller in Facsimile, Followed by the Four Voyages of Amerigo Vespucci, with their Translation into English; to which are added Waldseemüller's Two World Maps of 1507 with an Introduction*, ed. Charles George Hebermann (New York: United States Catholic Historical Society, 1907).

35 The seminal study of the *Sphere* is found in Lynn Thorndike, *The Sphere of Sacrobosco and its Commentators* (Chicago: University of Chicago Press, 1949).

36 First published in 1495, it was reprinted in 1499 and in 1500 in Venice and in Paris.

37 "Hic vertex nobis semper sublimis, at illum Sub pedibus Styx atra tenet Manesque profundi," *Georgics*, 1.242–43.

38 Pomponius Mela, *De Chorographia*, ed. Gunnar Ranstrand, Studia Graeca et Latina Gothoburgensia 28 (Gothenburg: Acta Universitatis Gothoburgensis, 1971).

39 Dionysius Periegetes, in *Geographi Graeci Minores*, 2 vols, ed. Karl Müller (Paris: Firmin-Didot, 1855–56), 2.103–76.

40 Alex Clairaut, "Exposition abrégée du système du monde, et explication des principaux phénomènes astronomiques tirée des Principes de M. Newton," supplement to the Marquise du Châtelet's translation of the *Principia* (Paris: Desaint & Saillant, 1756).

Translation of the
Cosmographiae Introductio

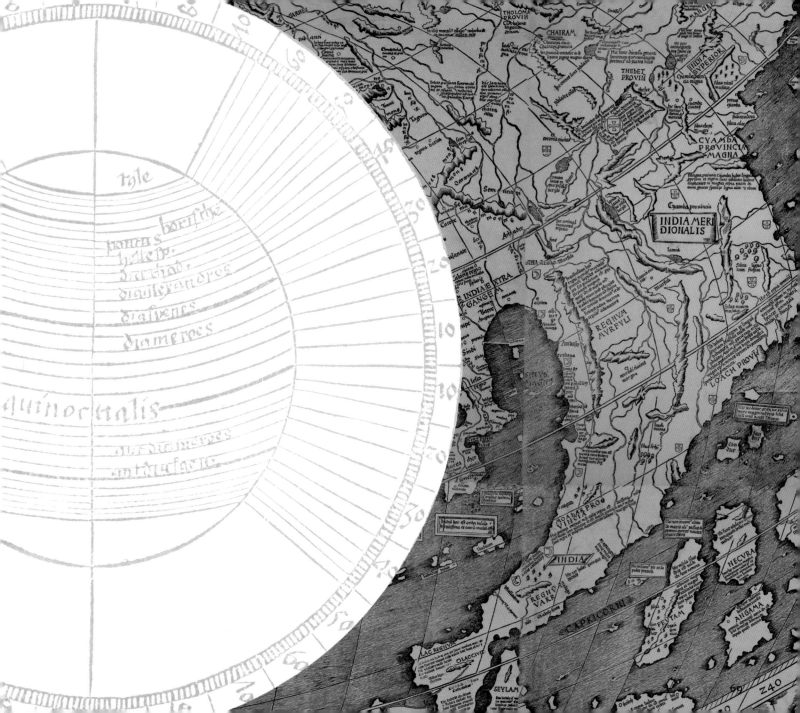

Introduction to Cosmography

containing the requisite principles of geometry and astronomy
beside the Four Voyages of Amerigo Vespucci

and

A proper representation of the whole world, both as a globe and a map,
that includes remote lands unknown to Ptolemy recently brought to light

Distichon[I]
Since god rules the stars and Caesar the earth
Neither the earth nor the stars hold them

For Maximilian Caesar Augustus[2]

From Philesius Vogesigena[3]

Since your Majesty is held sacred throughout the vast world,
Maximillian Caesar, in the most remote of lands,
Where the sun raises its golden face from the eastern seas
Searching for the straits known as Hercules,
Where the noon glows under its burning rays, and
Where the great bear freezes the surface of the sea,
To you the greatest of mighty kings who command
That just laws prevail,
In loyalty, we who have prepared it carefully
Dedicate this world map.

The End

For Maximilian Caesar Augustus

Martinus Ilacomilus[4]
wishes good fortune

Plato, Apollonius of Tyana[5] and many other philosophers who sought knowledge by traveling to the most distant lands have taught us that it is not only an enjoyable but also an important part of life to visit many lands and to see the farthest races of men. Their example gives us confidence, most invincible Maximilian Caesar, to say that few will deny that it is also profitable to learn from books[6] the location of lands, cities, and customs of foreign peoples,

> Which Phoebus sees when he buries his rays beneath the waves,
> After his rising in the farthest east,
> Those beneath the cold stare of the Bear
> And those burnt by the harsh south wind
> That bakes the hot dry sand.[7]

Who among men would deny that it is pleasant and profitable to learn from books the manners and customs of all these peoples? To express my own opinion, just as it is praiseworthy to travel far, it is also not foolish for one who knows the world from maps and books alone to repeat over and over the words from the *Odyssey* of Homer, the most learned of poets, the passage about Ulysses:

> Tell me, O Muse, of the man who after the capture of Troy
> Saw the customs and the cities of many men.[8]

Therefore, to the best of my ability I have studied with the help of others the books of Ptolemy from a Greek manuscript[9] and, having added the information from the four voyages of Amerigo Vespucci, I have drawn a map of the whole world for the general education of scholars as a way of introduction to cosmography, both as a globe and as a map. These works I am dedicating to you, since you are the lord of the known world. I feel certain that I shall accomplish what I have set forth if I know that I have satisfied in some way your correct judgment in such matters, and shall be safe from the intrigues of my critics as I work under your protection, as though under the shield of Achilles. Farewell, illustrious Caesar.
At St. Dié, in the year 1507 after the birth of Our Savior.

The Order of our Presentation

Because it is impossible for anyone to gain knowledge of cosmography without some small understanding of the discipline of astronomy, nor to gain knowledge of astronomy itself without knowing the basic principles of geometry, we will in this outline explain the order of the subjects to be presented in this book:

1. The elements of geometry that will be helpful in allowing a more comprehensive understanding of the sphere.

2. The meaning of the geometrical concepts of sphere, axis, poles, and definitions useful to cosmography.

3. The circles of the heavens.

4. The explanation of the theory of the sphere and how to divide it into degrees.

5. The meaning of the five celestial zones and their relationship to the system of degrees that divide up the heavens and the earth.

6. The theory of parallels on the earth.

7. The climatic zones that divide the earth.

8. The directions of the winds.

9. The presentation of the geographical divisions of the earth, the many seas, islands, and the distances of many places from one another.

We will add to this an explanation and diagram of a quadrant useful to the cosmographer and the book of the *Four Voyages of Amerigo Vespucci*. All this is presented in order to describe the cosmography that we have presented both as a globe and as a map.

Chapter *1*

The Elements of Geometry Necessary for a Comprehensive Notion of the Sphere

In this chapter Waldseemüller and Ringmann do not present a narrative in the usual sense but instead provide their readers with what appears to be a mere list of simple geometrical definitions. Although this information seems obvious, in the early sixteenth century the knowledge of geometry as written by Euclid was just beginning to filter into humanist circles through printed editions and commentaries, and would have been a necessary part of any text on cartography or astronomy. Waldseemüller sets out a group of definitions much in the style typical of books on astronomy and cartography of the period.

In the following pages we shall discuss concepts that require the knowledge of the circle, the circumference, the center, the diameter, and other similar geometric terms, and therefore, in order to provide a better understanding of these, briefly explain and define them one by one.

A circle is a plane figure surrounded by a line drawn completely around it with a point in the center such that all the straight lines drawn from it to the surrounding boundary line are of equal length to one another. A plane figure is one in which no point contained in the figure rises above or below the level of the lines that enclose the figure.

The circumference of the circle is the line that surrounds the figure in such a way that all the straight lines drawn to it through the center of the circle are equal in length to one another. This concept is also called *ambitus, circuitus, curvatura, circulus* and in Greek is known as the *periphereia*. The center of a circle is the point located so that all of the straight lines that can be drawn from it to the circumference are equal in length to one another.

A half-circle is a plane figure bounded by the diameter of the circle and half the circumference. The diameter of a circle is any straight line that passes through the center of the circle and extends in both directions to the circumference.

A straight line is the shortest distance that can be drawn between two points. An angle is the coming together of two lines. The angle is the portion of the intersection that increases in width as one moves away from the point of intersection. A right angle is an angle formed by one line falling upon another in such a way that the two angles made on either side are the same. If a right angle is formed by straight lines it is called plane. If the angle is formed by curved lines it is called spherical. An obtuse angle is any angle that is greater than a right angle. An acute angle is any angle that is less that a right angle.

A solid body can be measured by length, width and height. Each of these directions is equivalent.

A degree is a whole or part of an angle that is not the result of division of that thing into sixtieths. A minute is one-sixtieth part of a degree. A second is the sixtieth part of a minute. A third is the sixtieth part of a second, and continuing.

Chapter 2

The Meaning of the Geometrical Concepts of Sphere, Axis, Poles

Much of this chapter is taken up with expanding the definitions given in Chapter 1 to the solid sphere or the globe. The treatment of the geometry of the globe by Waldseemüller and Ringmann resembles in its essentials that given in the Sphere *of Sacrobosco, which was perhaps the most important text on astronomy in the late Middle Ages and early Renaissance. The other important astronomical textbook of the period, the* Novae Theoricae Planetarum *by Georg Peurbach (1423–61), was undoubtedly also well known to both Waldseemüller and Ringmann, and this chapter was heavily influenced by both works.*

In order to easily understand the description of the whole world as handed down through the years by Ptolemy, it is necessary to have knowledge of the solid or material sphere. Once this is understood, a better view of the world enlarged by later scholars and the new discoveries of Amerigo Vespucci will be possible.

A sphere[10] (as defined by Theodosius[11] in his book on spheres) is a solid figure bounded by a convex surface, in the center of which there exists a point such that all of the straight lines drawn from this point to the surface are equal to one another. According to many modern writers there are ten celestial spheres, but the eighth sphere is fixed because it carries the fixed stars and is composed of circles joined together ideally by a line and axis crossing the center that is occupied by the earth.

The axis of a sphere is a line passing through the center and intersecting at the farthest points on both sides of the circumference of the sphere. Around this axis the spheres rotate much like the wheel of a wagon about the axle, which in the case of the sphere is a smoothly rounded pole. On this subject Manilius speaks as follows:

> Through the cold air an invisible line is drawn;
> Around it the starry world revolves.[12]

The poles, which are called the *cardines,*[13] and the vertices terminate the axis of the sphere and are points that never move. Our explanation of the axis and poles of the material sphere are referred to the eighth sphere because it resembles it as a limited version. On the material sphere there are two principal poles, one the northern, also called Arcticus and Borealis, the other the southern, called Antarcticus.[14] Hence Virgil says:

> One pole is ever high above us
> While the other, beneath our feet,
> Is seen of black Styx and shades infernal.[15]

The arctic pole is always seen by those who live in Europe and in Asia and is named the *Arctus* or *Arcturus*, after the Great Bear which is also named *Calisto, Helice,* and *Septentrionalis* from the seven stars of *Plaustrum,*[16] that are called Triones. There are also seven stars in the Minor Bear, which is at times called Cynosura.[17] In speaking of these constellations Baptista Mantuanus[18] says:

> Under your guidance, Helice, under yours Cynosura,
> We set sail over the deep waters.

The wind coming from that part of the world is named in the same way and is called Borealis and Aquilonicus. Many sailors call Cynosura the star of the sea.

On the opposite side of the earth from the northern pole is the Antarctic, and it derives its name from the Greek *anti*, which means the same thing as *contra* in Latin. The southern pole also goes by the names Noticus and Austronoticus. The southern pole cannot be observed by us because of the curvature of the earth that slopes downward, but the pole is visible from the antipodes (the existence of which has been established).

Chapter 3

The Circles of the Heavens

Although Waldseemüller and Ringmann have explained many of the geometrical definitions that form the basis for cartography as will be discussed in the Cosmographiae Introductio, *they still expected their readers to know something about Ptolemy and the assumptions that underlie his* Geography. *In this way the* Introductio *presents difficulties for the modern reader that would not have been experienced by readers in the early sixteenth century. In the following chapter Waldseemüller lays out the structure of the imaginary lines that were used by Ptolemy and all Greek astronomers to mark the earth and allow distances to be calculated in relation to the stars. Although the names of these lines representing the tropics, the equator and the zodiac are still in use today, their basis as imaginary reference points in the celestial sphere is not well known. We must remember that in the early sixteenth century the earth was still thought of as the center of the cosmos and the lines of the tropics, the equator, the Arctic and Antarctic circles, and the zodiac are projected down to the earth from the celestial sphere above. From these lines the equinoxes and summer and winter solstices were calculated assuming that the sun and stars revolved around the earth.*

There are two kinds of imaginary circles, called *segmina* by many authors, in the heavens, the great and the small.[19] A great circle is one which, inscribed on the surface of the sphere, divides it into two equal parts. There are six great circles: the equator, the zodiac, the equinoctial, the solstitial, the meridian and the horizon. A small circle is one that when inscribed on the same surface of the sphere divides it into two unequal parts. There are four small circles: the arctic, the tropic of Capricorn, the tropic of Cancer and Antarctic. There are then ten circles in all.

The equator (also called the belt of the equinoctial) is a great circle dividing the sphere into two parts. Any point on the circle of the equator is equally distant from both poles. It is called this because when the sun crosses it, it is the equinox throughout the world and the length of the day and the night are equal. The equinox that occurs in March or of the constellation Aries is the vernal equinox; the equinox in September or of the constellation Libra is the autumnal.

The zodiac[20] is a great circle that intersects the equator at two points, which are the first points of Aries and Libra. One half of this circle inclines to the north, the other inclines to the south. The name derives either from the Greek *zodion,* that means animal, because it contains the figures of twelve animals in it, or from *zoe,* meaning life, because the lives of all those on earth are governed by the motion of the planets. In Latin it is called the sign bearer because it has twelve signs in it. It is an oblique circle.[21] Virgil says of it:

Where the slanting array of Signs may turn.

In the middle of the zodiac there is a circular line dividing it in two and leaving six degrees on either side. That line is called the ecliptic and no eclipse of the sun or of the moon ever takes place unless both of these bodies pass under that line in the same or in opposite degrees. In the same direction we see an eclipse of the sun, while in the opposite it is an eclipse of the moon.[22] During its movement the sun always passes with its center under the ecliptic and never deviates from it. The rest of the planets and the moon wander from one side to the other.

There are two colures[23] or tropics on the sphere that go by the names solstitial and equinoctial. They are called colures from the Greek word *colon,* and the word for wild oxen (Caesar in his commentaries says that they are found in the Hercynian forest the size of elephants).[24] They are called this because just as the tail of the wild oxen inscribes a semicircle when it begins to move, so the line of the colure is only half-visible and even though it is a great circle it appears to us as incomplete.

The solstitial colure, also called the circle of declinations, is a great circle that passes through the first points of the constellations of Cancer and Capricorn and also through the poles of the ecliptic and the poles of the earth. In very much the same way, the equinoctial colure passes through the first points of the constellations of Aries and Libra and also through the poles of the earth.

A meridian is a great circle passing through a point that is directly overhead and through the poles of the world. Relating to our own representation of the world we have drawn these circles every ten degrees on the flat map and the globe. Over everything there is a point directly above it in the sky called the zenith.

The great circle of the horizon (the limiting line) divides the upper part of the sphere from the lower. It is the circle which the view of those who stand under an open sky see coming to an end and separating the part of the heavens that can be seen from that which cannot be seen. The limit of the horizon line varies from location to location, the pole being the point directly overhead every horizon.[25] Now that we have considered the names and uses of the great circles let us move on to the lesser ones.

The Arctic Circle is a small circle that one pole of the zodiac describes by the motion of the prime mover.[26] The Antarctic is a small circle that the other pole of the zodiac makes by revolving around that pole of the world. The pole of the zodiac is a point that is equally distant from any point on the ecliptic. The poles of the zodiac are the farthest points of the axis of the ecliptic. The distance of this pole from the pole of the earth is equal to the greatest declination of the sun.

The tropic of Cancer is a lesser circle by which the sun, when at the first point of that constellation, describes the motion of the prime mover. This point is called the summer solstice. The tropic of Capricorn is a lesser circle by which the sun, when at the first point of that constellation, describes the motion of the prime mover. This is the circle of the winter solstice.

Because we have talked about it, it must be noted, that declination occurs when the sun descends from the equinoctial to the tropic of Cancer or from where we are located to the tropic of Capricorn. Ascension occurs in the contrary fashion when the sun approaches the equator from the direction of the tropics. It is not correct, as some have written, that the sun ascends when it nears us and descends when it moves away.

Until now we have written only of circles. Let us carefully proceed now to the theory of the sphere and a consideration of the measure by which such circles are distant from each other.

Chapter 4

The Theory of the Sphere and How to Divide it into Degrees

In this chapter Waldseemüller and Ringmann describe the actual locations on the earth of the imaginary lines discussed in the previous chapter. They give the locations of the tropics and the equator, and talk about the path of the zodiac in order to lay the foundations for the division of the earth into zones and degrees. They will have more to say about these zones in the coming chapters.

As we have shown, the celestial sphere is surrounded by five principal circles, one great and four small: the Arctic, the circle of Cancer, the equator, the circle of Capricorn, and the Antarctic. Many authors call the spaces that are between these circles zones. Virgil for example in the *Georgics* says:

> Five zones comprise the heavens, one is always glowing with the burning sun,
> Always scorched by his flames.
> Around this two at the world's ends, stretching right and left,
> Set fast in ice and black storms.
> Between these two and the middle zone,
> by the gods' goodness given to feeble mortals,
> A path is cut between the two wherein the slanting array of Signs may turn.[27]

We will say more on the nature of these zones later in our book. Because we have described the pole that defines the Arctic Circle it must be understood for our further explanation that by this we mean the upper pole of the zodiac situated at an elevation of 66°9′ and distant from the pole of the earth by 24°51′.[28] One should recall from our treatment that a degree is a thirtieth part of a sign of the zodiac and that a sign is one-twelfth of a circle. Multiplying these together gives 360, hence it is easy to see that a degree can be defined as the 360th part of a full circle.

The lower pole of the zodiac describes the Antarctic Circle, which is situated in the same degree of declination and is at the same distance from the lower pole of the earth as is the upper pole of the zodiac. The greatest declination of the sun toward the north, which is the other inclination of the ecliptic, is situated at 33°51′[29] and describes the tropic of Cancer. The inclination towards the south describing the tropic of Capricorn is the greatest declination of the sun towards the south. The distance between the Arctic Circle and the tropic of Cancer is the same as the distance between the tropic of Capricorn and the Antarctic Circle, 42°18′. In the middle of the heavens lies the equator equally distant from the poles of the world.

To briefly discuss the other circles we begin with the zodiac that is determined by its poles. From the poles to the tropics the distance is 42°18′ and the width of the zodiac is 6° from the ecliptic toward each of the tropics, or 12° in all.

The solstices and the equinoxes define the colures of declination and of ascension that intersect under the poles of the earth along the axis of the heavens at spherical right angles. But the equinoctial colures that lie along the zodiac make oblique angles and make right angles along the zodiac of the solstices. The movable meridian circle is contained by the same axis as the poles of the earth themselves.

The circle that is the horizon is determined by the zenith that is its upper pole and is a point equally distant from all points on it. The circle of the horizon divides the hemispheres of the earth into east and west, but for those who live beneath the equinoctial, it goes through the two poles of the world. The zenith point of every possible horizon is always a fourth of a circle, 90°, and the circumference of the horizon is four times the distance between the zenith and the horizon.

We should take notice that the axis of the earth in the solid sphere passes from the poles through the center of the world along a diameter. The axis of the zodiac is imaginary and, not being part of the material sphere, it must therefore be conceived of by the mind. This line intersects the center of the axis of the world and makes unequal angles with the axis of the earth.

Conceived of in the way we have just presented, we find that there seems to be a wonderful order and extraordinary arrangement of things in the very way that the world was created. The ancient astronomers, having described the form of the world, comprehended and followed in the footsteps of the Creator himself. He who made all things did so according to quantity using number, weight and dimensions. We, who have chosen in this book to present our system using the complicated method of degrees and minutes, realize the difficulty in comprehending this subject and shall simplify it by only using the values of degrees in full. In our treatment and in other books on the sphere there is not much difference between 51′ and the measure of a full degree 60′.[30] Therefore in the figure (figure 1) that we have inserted below to provide a better understanding of these complex matters, the tropics of Capricorn and Cancer and the greatest declinations of the sun will be located at distance of 24° from the equinoctial. This is the same distance as the poles of the zodiac or the Arctic from the poles of the earth, situated at an elevation of over 66°.

& capricorni/ atꝗ maximę ſolis declinationes ab
ęquinoctiali.2ꝗ. gradibus diſtabūt. Quantū & po͛
li ipſius'zodiaci/ſiue circuli arcticus & ātarcticus a
polis mundi ſunt diſtantes ſuper ſexageſimū ſextū
eleuationis gradum ſiti.

Polus Arcticus

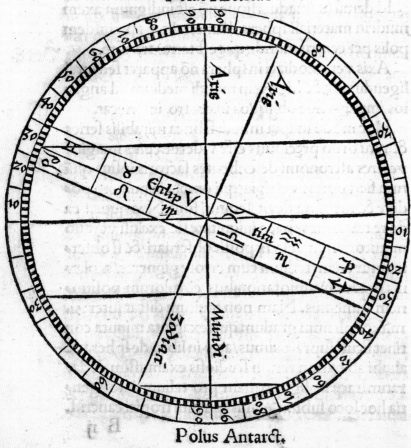

Polus Antarct.

Chapter 5

The Meaning of the Five Celestial Zones and their Relationship to the System of Degrees that Divide up the Heavens and the Earth

In this chapter Waldseemüller and Ringmann proceed to divide the earth into five zones as did Ptolemy and many other ancient geographers. The celestial zones are defined by the imaginary circles discussed in earlier chapters. These zones are distinguished from each other by temperature and habitability. Waldseemüller tells us that the temperate ones are inhabited and makes a distinction between those zones that are very cold and those that have unbearable heat. He provides an explanatory figure that is a schematic of his model of the earth as has been presented to the reader thus far. In this chapter Waldseemüller also tells us for the first time of the hot and torrid lands in the far south that have been recently discovered by Amerigo Vespucci.

So far in our little book we have spoken of many geometrical principles and outlined the form of the sphere, of the poles, of the five zones, of the circles that surround the world and of the particular theory of the earth that stems from these principles. We come now to the application of the principles of the circles and of the degrees to the earth. We have placed the discussion of the earth here in an order, which if I am not mistaken, can be easily comprehended by the reader. It should therefore be known to the reader that on the earth there are five regions that correspond to the zones that we presented earlier. Of these zones Ovid in the *Metamorphoses* says:

> And as there are two zones on the right and two on the left
> That divide the heavens, and a fifth zone between,
> So did the providence of the god mark out what they enclose
> With the same number, and just as many regions are marked upon the earth.
> Of these the middle cannot be inhabited by reason of extreme heat,
> Deep snow covers two, and two he placed in between with temperate climate
> Mingling the hot with the cold.[31]

RVDIMENTA

Quarta quę par eſt /totidem
Quinta ỹo torrida & media gradus .27. &.92; mi;
Sed horũ quendam typum ponamus;

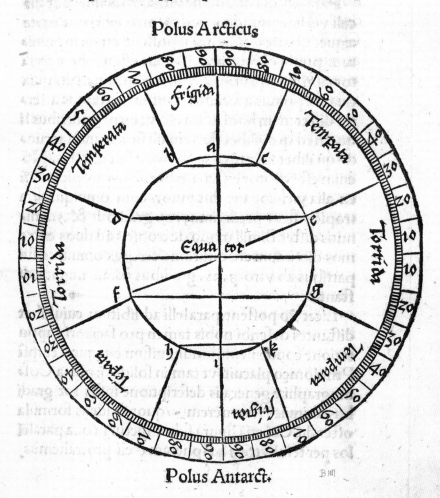

Polus Arcticus

frigida

Temperata

Temperata

Torrida

Torrida

Equator

Temperata

Torrida

frigida

Polus Antarct.

B iij

Fig 2.

Representation of the five climatic zones

A schematic representation of the earth showing the nomenclature that Waldseemüller and Ringmann will use in their description of the climatic zones that divide up the earth. The division of the earth's surface into climatic zones in the *Cosmographiae Introductio* follows that of Ptolemy and separates the earth into inhabitable and uninhabitable regions based on temperature.

Courtesy of the Rare Book and Special Collections Division, Library of Congress

Let us say, in order to make this matter easier for our readers to understand, that the four small circles – the Arctic, the circle of Cancer, the circle of Capricorn, and the Antarctic – separate and divide the earth and the heavens into the five zones. In the following diagram (figure 2) let *a* stand for the Arctic pole of the earth, *bc* the circle of the arctic, *de* the circle of Cancer, *fg* the circle of Capricorn, *hk* the Antarctic circle, and *i* the south pole.

The first zone called the Arctic comprises all of the space between *bac*. This zone is eternally frozen and perpetually cold and is therefore uninhabited. The second zone is a temperate zone and is inhabited. It occupies the space between *bc* and *de*.

The third zone is all of the space included between *de* and *fg*. Because of the amount of heat this zone is barely habitable. The sun describes circles in this zone with a constant motion along the line *fe*, which marks the ecliptic, and by reason of the excessive heat makes the zone torrid and uninhabited. The fourth zone is all the space included between *fg* and *hk*. This is a temperate zone and is habitable if the vast areas of water and the changing conditions of the air permit it. The fifth zone comprises all the space between *hkl*. This zone is always frozen with cold and uninhabited.[32]

It should be understood that when we say that a zone of the heavens is either inhabited or uninhabited we mean that this applies to the corresponding zone on the earth that lies beneath the celestial zone. When we say that a zone is inhabited or habitable we mean that it is easy to live there. When a zone is difficult to live in we likewise say that it is uninhabited or uninhabitable. There are many peoples who inhabit the hot and dry torrid zone, such as the inhabitants of the Golden Chersonese,[33] the Taprobanenses,[34] the Ethiopians, and of a very large part of the earth that for all time was unknown, but has been recently discovered by Amerigo Vespucci. Because of his discovery we shall add to this book an account of his four voyages translated from the Italian language into French and from French into Latin.

Chapter 6

The Theory of Parallels on the Earth

The theory of parallels that Waldseemüller and Ringmann present here is that of Ptolemy and is based on time increments of the longest day. Ptolemy's selection of a sequence of unequally spaced parallels defined by the length of day instead of parallels of equal spacing at uniform intervals reflects the traditional practice of Greek geography. Latitudes and parallels defined in this way become more crowded the farther we move from the equator. Although Waldseemüller presents Ptolemy's system he chooses instead to employ a system of regularly spaced parallels on the 1507 World Map. This is one of the only places where the text of the book diverges from the map. Waldseemüller probably found that when mapping a greatly enlarged world, much of which lay far from the equator, using Ptolemy's system of parallels led to confusions when laying out the map.

Parallels[35] or almucantars[36] are circles or lines that are equidistant in every direction and at every point and that never intersect even if extended to infinity. They bear the same relationship to each other as the circle of the equator bears to the four small circles on the earth. The second parallel is not, however, as distant from the third as the first is from the second. It will be clear from what is explained in the following pages, however, that if any two circles that represent parallels are joined by a perpendicular, they will be equally distant from each other throughout their extent. For the equator is neither closer nor farther from one of the tropics at any one point than at any other, since it is everywhere at a distance of 23°51′ from the tropics as we have explained before. The same can be said of the distance from the tropics to the extreme circles, for they are both 42°44′[37] from the nearer tropic at every point.

For even though parallels can be drawn at any distance apart, we have decided, as did Ptolemy, in our representation of the universe, both as a globe and as a map, to separate the parallels from one another as the following table shows.[38] To this table we have added a diagram (figure 3[39]) in which the parallels that we have constructed through the earth extend to the celestial sphere.

Paralelli ab ęquat.	gradus cœli	Horę dierũ ma.	Quot millia. gra. vnus
21 Diatiles 8	63	20	28.½
20	61	19	
19	58	18	32.½
18	56	17	½
17	54	17	37.½
16 Diarhip.7	51.½	16.½	40.½
15 Diabor.6	48.½	16	42.½
14	45	15.½	44
13	43.1/12	15.¼	45
12 Diarho.5	40.½.⅓.1/12	15	47
11	38.½.1/12	14.½.¼	48.½
10 Diarho.4	36	14.½	50
9	33.⅓	14.¼	
8 Diaalex.3	30.⅓	14	54
7	27.½.⅙	13.½.¼	
6 Diasienes 2	23.½.⅓	13.½	57
5	20.¼	13.¼	
4 Diamero.1	16.⅓.1/12	13	
3	12.½	12.½.¼	
2	8.⅓.1/12	12.½	
1	4.¼	12.¼	59
Aeq̃tor a polis eq̃distans		12 cõtinuę	60
1	4.¼	12.¼	59
2	8.⅓.1/12	12.½	
3	12.2	12.½.¼	
4 Diameroes.	16.⅓.12	13	
5	20.¼.	13.¼	

Climata cũ gradibus paralellorũ simul horas Insinuat numeris ista figura suis.

a

Fig 3.

Table of parallels and schematic diagram

The surface of the earth according to Ptolemy is divided up into parallels (lines of latitude) that are spaced according to the length of the longest day. This system produces parallels that are not equally spaced as is the case on modern maps. In this table of parallels and schematic diagram opposite, Waldseemüller describes the Ptolemaic and traditional Greek system of parallels even though he employs a more modern equidistant system of lines on the 1507 map.

Courtesy of the Rare Book and Special Collections Divison, Library of Congress

Para. & cli.	Gradus	Horę	Milliaria
6 Antidiasienes	23.$\frac{11}{23}$	13.$\frac{1}{2}$	52
7	27.$\frac{1}{2}\frac{1}{6}$	13.$\frac{1}{2}\frac{1}{8}$	

Et ita deinceps ỹsus Antarcticum polũ. Quod
& subsequens figura cõmonstrat.

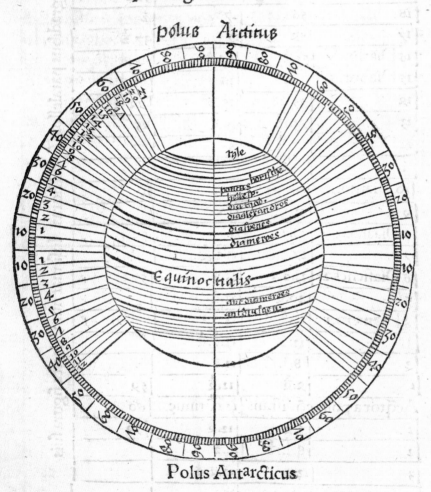

Chapter 7

The Climatic Zones that Divide the Earth

Even though the circles that divide the earth are primarily of astronomical origin, ancient geographers used them to divide the earth into geographical and climatic zones. Waldseemüller and Ringmann, following Ptolemy, define a group of climatic zones using the system of parallels that he has just laid out in the previous chapter. The layout of the zones for Waldseemüller is symmetrical about the equator. He will quote from several ancient geographers in describing the inhabitants of these zones, and most significantly it is in this chapter that we first learn of the naming of America after Amerigo Vespucci.

Even though the word *climata* is defined as a region, it will be used here to represent a part of the earth that lies between two equidistant parallels lying from the beginning to the end at a difference in half-hour intervals of the longest day at each parallel. The number of any climate starting from the equator indicates the number of half-hours by which the longest day in that climate exceeds the day that is equal to the night. There exist seven of these climates, although the seventh climate toward the south has yet to be explored.[40] But toward the north, Ptolemy describes a country that was both habitable and comfortable at a distance of seven and a half hours. The seven climates are named by the prominent city, river or mountain that is their limit.

Climate 1
The first climate is called *Dia Meroes*, from the Greek *dia*, which means "through" and defines in that language the genitive case, and Meroe, which is a city in Africa located in the torrid zone 16° on this side of the equator along the same parallel on which the Nile River is found. On our world map [see Introduction, figure 2] for the clearer understanding of which this book was written, we will clearly show the extent of the first climate and also of the rest, as well as the number of hours of the longest day in each of them.[41]

Climate 2
Dia Sienes derives from Syene, a city in Egypt and the beginning of the region of Thebais.

Climate 3

Dia Alexandrias, from Alexandria, a famous city in Africa, the most important city in Egypt, founded by Alexander the Great, of whom the poet said, "for the Pellean youth one globe is not enough."[42]

Climate 4

Dia Rhodon, from Rhodes, an island on the coast of Asia Minor, on which in our time there is situated a famous city of the same name that valiantly resisted the vicious attacks of the Turks and gloriously sent them back.

Climate 5

Dia Rome, from a well-known city of Europe, the most glorious of the cities of Italy and at one time in history the most famous conqueror of all nations and capital of the world. It is now the home of the mighty Father of all Fathers.

Climate 6

Dia Borysthenes, from the large river of the Scythians, the fourth-largest river after the Danube.

Climate 7

Dia Rhipheon, from the Riphaean Mountains, a large range in Salmatian Europe, always white and covered with snow.

Using these prominent places, through which the meridian lines that border the climates pass, Ptolemy derived the names of the seven climates.

Ptolemy did not discuss the eighth climate because that part of the earth was unknown to him but was explored by later scholars. It is called *Dia Tyles* because the beginning of the climate located on the twenty-first parallel from the equator passes directly through Thule. Thule is an island in the far north about which Virgil says,

While farthest Thule serves.[43]

We must now speak of all of the climates that lie to the south of the equator, six of which have corresponding names. These have been explored and may be called *Antidia Meroes* from the Greek *anti*, which means opposite or against. The farthest part of Africa, the islands of Zanzibar, the lesser Java, and Seula and the fourth part of the earth are all situated in the sixth climate towards Antarctica. The fourth part of the earth we have decided to call Amerige, the land of Amerigo we might even say, or America because it was discovered by Amerigo. Pomponius Mela, the geographer, writing of these southern climates, says:

> The habitable zones have the same seasons, but at different times of the year. The Antichthones inhabit the one,[44] and we the other. The situation of the former zone being unknown because of the heat of the intervening expanse, the geography of the latter is now to be described. [45]

We shall say here that each one of the climates produces products of different types, in as much as the climates vary in character and are controlled by the stars in different ways. Virgil says of the differences:

> Nor can all climates all fruits of the earth produce.
> Here springs the corn and here the grape;
> Elsewhere earth is green with the tender growth of trees
> And grass unchecked. See how from Tmolus comes the
> Saffron's fragrance, ivory from Ind,
> From Sabaean's feeble sons their frankincense,
> Iron from the naked Chalybes, rank beaver oil
> From Pontus, from Epirus the prize-palms of the mares of Elis. [46]

Chapter 8

The Directions of the Winds

Once again following Ptolemy, Waldseemüller and Ringman lay out a system of directions based on twelve winds. Four of these correspond to the cardinal directions of the compass. The remainder of the winds are spaced at 30-degree intervals. The angular distribution of the winds was used by many ancient geographers to specify directions for sailing.

In the preceding pages of our book we have mentioned the winds that blow across the earth now when we spoke of the North and South Pole. It is of course well known that some understanding of the winds is helpful and can be of great importance to cosmography. We shall for this reason say something in this chapter about the winds, the *spiritus* and the *flatus*. Wind as is known by the philosophers is an exhalation, a blowing, that can be both warm and dry or cold and wet as it moves across the surface of the earth.[47]

Now, because the sun has a triple rising and setting (the equinoctial, the winter and the summer) according to its relationship to the two tropics and to the equator and because of the fact that there are two sides of the equator, one to the north and the other to the south, each of these directions has winds peculiar to them. Therefore, it naturally follows that there are twelve winds in all, three from the east, three from the north, three from the south and three from the west. The four winds that are shown in the diagram (figure 4) occupy the middle place and are primary, whereas the others are considered secondary.

The poets, however, in the spirit of creativity and according to tradition, talk of the secondary winds, which they also call side winds.[48] Thus Ovid says:

> Eurus retreated to the dawn, to the Nabatean realms,
> To Persia and the mountains beneath the morning rays;
> The evening and the shores warmed by the setting sun
> Are nearest to Zephyrus; Sythia and the seven Oxen
> Are seized by icy Boreas; the land directly opposite
> Is drenched with constant clouds and rain by Auster.'[49]

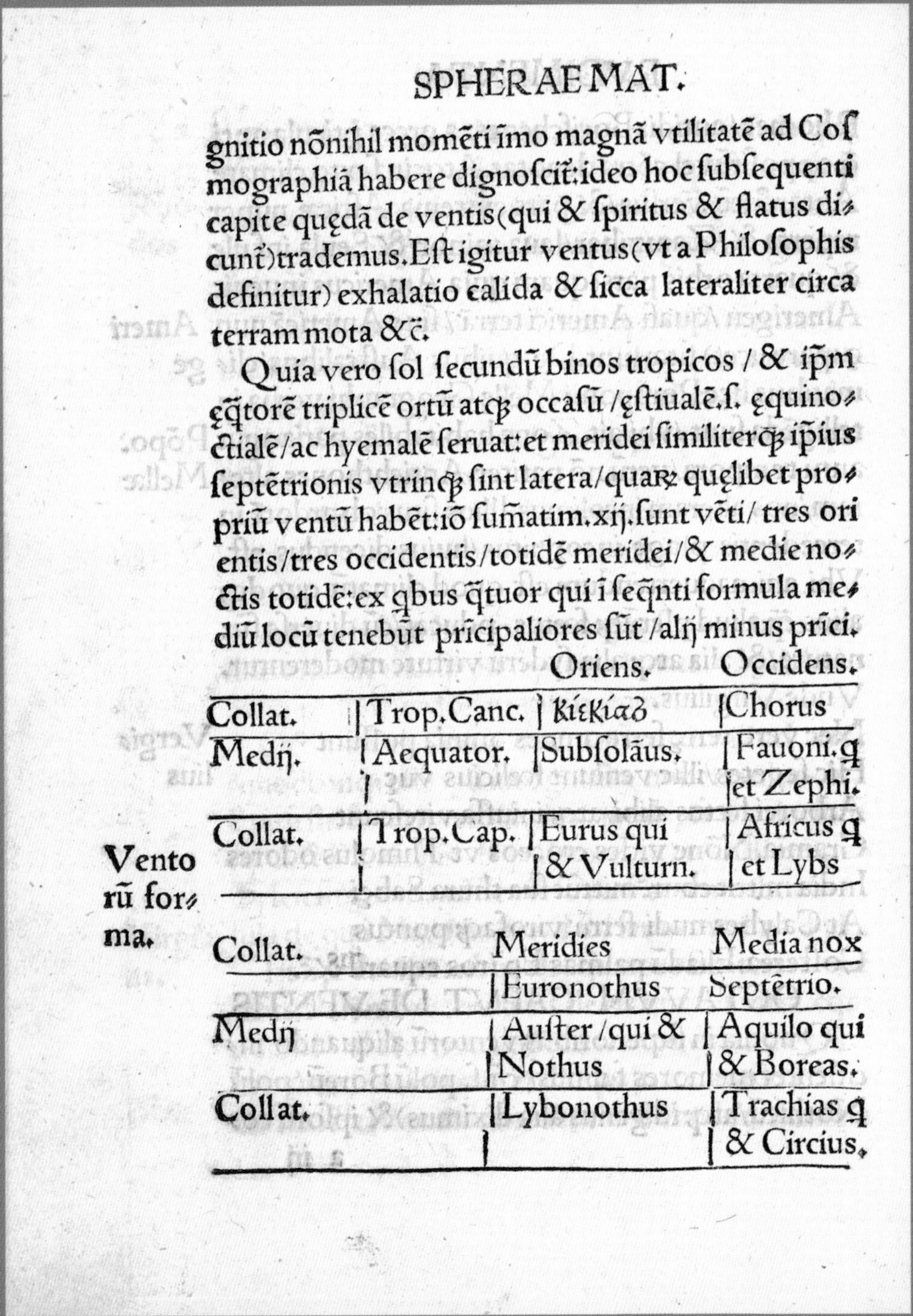

gnitio nõnihil mõmeti imo magnã vtilitatê ad Cof
mographiã habere dignoscit:ideo hoc subsequenti
capite quedã de ventis(qui & spiritus & flatus di
cunt)trademus.Est igitur ventus(vt a Philosophis
definitur) exhalatio calida & sicca lateraliter circa
terram mota &c̃.

Quia vero sol secundũ binos tropicos / & ipm̃
ẽqtorê triplicê ortũ atcq̃ occasũ /ẽstiualẽ.s. equino
ctialẽ/ac hyemalẽ seruat:et meridei similitercq̃ ipius
septẽtrionis vtrincq̃ sint latera/quaz quẽlibet pro
priũ ventũ habẽt:io sumãtim.xij.sunt vẽti/ tres ori
entis/tres occidentis/totidẽ meridei/& medie no
ctis totidẽ:ex qbus q̃tuor qui i seq̃nti formula me
diũ locũ tenebũt pricipaliores sũt /alij minus prici.

Fig 4.

Table of winds

Table showing the names of the primary winds used in the *Cosmographiae Introductio*. The four major winds blow in directions that correspond to the cardinal compass points.

Courtesy of the Rare Book and Special Collections Divison, Library of Congress

			Oriens.		Occidens.
	Collat.	Trop.Canc.	κίϵκίαδ		Chorus
	Medij.	Aequator.	Subsolãus.		Fauoni. q̃ et Zephi.
	Collat.	Trop.Cap.	Eurus qui & Vulturn.		Africus q̃ et Lybs
Vento rũ for ma.			Meridies		Media nox
				Euronothus	Septẽtrio.
	Medij		Auster /qui & Nothus		Aquilo qui & Boreas.
	Collat.		Lybonothus		Trachias q̃ & Circius.

The east wind is made purer and finer by the rays of the sun than all the others and as a result is very healthful. The west wind, having a mixture of heat and moisture, can melt the snows. Hence Virgil's verse says:

> In the dawning spring when icy streams trickle from snowy mountains,
> and the crumbling clod breaks at Zephyrus' touch.[50]

The south wind shuttles storms, great waves and rain. Of it Ovid says:

> Forth flies Notus with dripping wings.[51]

The north wind, because it is severely cold, freezes the waters.

> And the frosty winter with his north wind the sea face rough does wear.[52]

In regard to these winds, I can recall the verses of our poet Gallinarius,[53] a man of great learning, composed as follows:

> Eurus and Subsolanus blow from the east,
> Zephyrus and Favonius fill the west with breezes,
> Auster and Notus rage on Libya's farthest shore,
> Boreas and Aquilo cloud-dispelling threaten from the north.

Although the winds from the north are by their nature cold, they are warmed as they pass through the torrid zone. This has also been found to be true of the south wind, which passes through the torrid zone before it reaches us as is written in the following lines:

> Wherever the cold south wind blows it rages and binds the waters tightly.
> But until the cold blast passes through the torrid regions of the earth, it
> comes welcome to our home shores and hurls back the merciless gales of

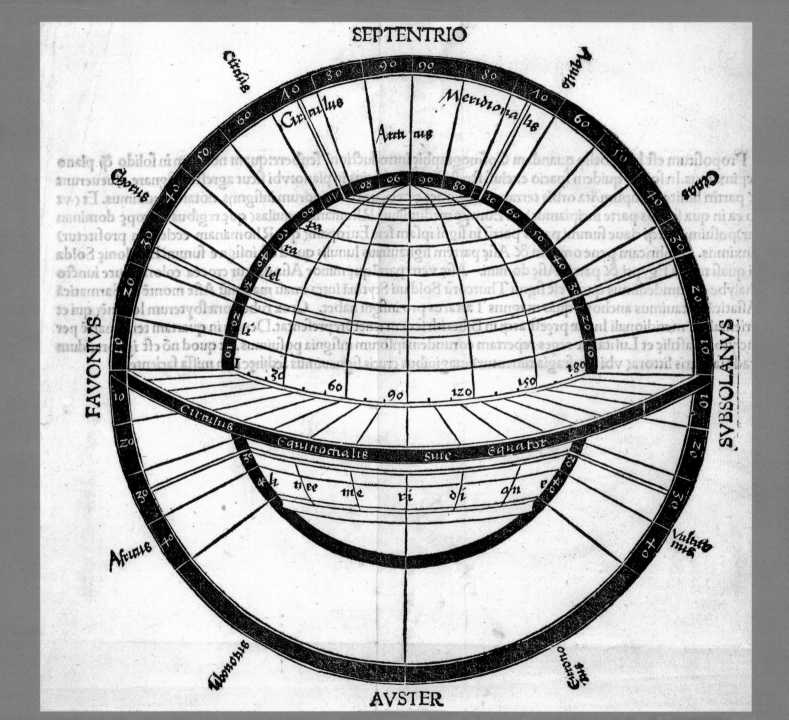

Fig 5.

Overall plan of the map

This figure is a fold-out page in the actual text of the *Cosmographiae Introductio* and is meant to be a summary of the information that has been provided by Waldseemüller and Ringmann thus far in their introduction to Cosmography. The figure shows the layout of the great circles on the surface of the earth, a system of lines that describe both longitude and latitude and the directions of the winds.

Courtesy of the Rare Book and Special Collections Divison, Library of Congress

the north wind. The latter wind deals harshly with us, weakens as it goes along and becomes gentler in the lowest part of the earth. The other change as they travel their various courses and have a nature proper to their origins.

Having said this about the winds, we now insert a schematic map (figure 5)[54], showing the poles, the axes, the circles, great as well as lesser, the five zones, the degrees of latitude and longitude, both on the earth and the heavens that we have discussed here.

Chapter 9

Rudiments of Cosmography:
The Presentation of the Geographical Divisions of the Earth, the Many Seas, Islands, and the Distances of Many Places From One Another

In perhaps the most important of all the chapters in the Cosmographiae Introductio, *Waldseemüller and Ringman here discuss the discovery of the New World, tell us that it is an island and reasserts that it was discovered by Amerigo Vespucci. This chapter includes his comments about new sailing charts and the shape of South America that have fueled much debate and speculation surrounding the 1507 World Map. It is perhaps one of the most intriguing pieces of prose written in the history of cartography. Waldseemüller uses quotes from several ancient geographers and develops a view of the world out of the classical tradition of Ptolemy that is at once radical and also surprisingly modern.*

The whole earth is but a point in comparison with the vastness of the entire heavens. This fact is of course well known from astronomical observations. Therefore, if the earth's circumference is compared to the size of the celestial sphere, it may be thought of as having absolutely no extent. There is at this time a fourth part of this small world barely[55] known to Ptolemy and inhabited by beings like ourselves. Previously, it was divided into only three parts: Europe, Africa and Asia.

Europe is bounded on the western side by the Atlantic Ocean, on the northern side by the British Ocean, on the eastern side by the river Tanais,[56] Lake Maeotis, and the Black Sea, and on the southern side by the Mediterranean Sea. It includes Spain, Gaul, Germany, Raetia,[57] Italy, Greece, and Sarmatia. Europe is named after Europa, the daughter of King Agenor. While playing along the seashore accompanied by her maidens from Tyre, Europa is believed to have been carried off by Jupiter, who assumed the character of a snow-white bull. She was brought over the sea while riding on his back and he gave her name to land lying opposite that island.

Africa is bounded on the west by the Atlantic Ocean, on the south by the Ethiopian Ocean, on the north by the Mediterranean Sea, and on the east by the Nile River. It embraces the Mauritanias, Tingitana[58] and Caesarea,[59] inland Libya, Numidia, lesser Africa that contains Carthage the historic rival of the Roman Empire, Cyrenaica,[60] Marmarica, inland Ethiopia, Egypt and others. It is called Africa because it is spared the severity of the cold.[61]

Asia, a land much larger than the other divisions in size and in wealth, is separated from Europe by the river Tanias and from Africa by an isthmus, which stretches to the south and divides the Arabian and Egyptian seas. The principal countries of Asia are Bithynia,[62] Galatia,[63] Cappadocia, Pamphylia,[64] Lydia, Cilicia,[65] greater and lesser Armenia, Colchis,[66] Hyrcania,[67] Ibernia, and Albania, along with many other lands that would take too long for us to mention. Asia is named after the queen of the same name.

Today these parts of the earth have been more extensively explored than a fourth part of the world, as will be explained in what follows, and that has been discovered by Amerigo Vespucci. Because it is well known that Europe and Asia were named after women, I can see no reason why anyone would have good reason to object to calling this fourth part Amerige, the land of Amerigo, or America, after the man of great ability who discovered it. The location of this part and the customs of its people can be clearly understood from the four voyages of Amerigo Vespucci that we have placed after this introduction.

The earth is now known to be divided into four parts. The first three of these are connected and are continents, but the fourth part is an island because it has been found[68] to be completely surrounded on all of its sides by sea. Just as there is only one earth, there is only one Ocean,[69] yet it is made up of many different seas and filled with many islands that go by different names. These names may be found in our Cosmography and in Priscian,[70] who in his translation of Dionysius[71] recounts them in the following lines:

The vast abyss of the ocean, however, surrounds the earth on every side. But the Ocean, although there is only one, takes many names. In the western countries it is called the Atlantic Ocean, but in the north, where the

Arimaspi[72] are ever warring, it is called sluggish or the Saturnian sea and by some the Dead Sea. [...][73] Where, however, the sun rises with its first light they call it the Eastern or Indian Sea. But where the inclined pole receives the hot south wind, it is called the Ethiopian or the Red Sea. [...]

As was said above therefore, a great ocean known by many names encircles the vast world. [...]

With its reach the first stretches out and separates Spain with its waves extending to the shores of Libya all the way to the coast of Pamphylia. The area is smaller than the rest of the gulfs. A larger gulf is one that enters the Caspian land and that receives its large watery flow from the vast ocean of the north. The arm of the sea that Tethys rules as the Saturnian sea is called the Caspian or the Hyrcanian. But the two gulfs that come from the south sea, one, the Persian running northward, forms a deep sea, lying opposite the country where the waters of the Caspian roll, while the other beats upon the shores of Panchaea[74] and extends to the south opposite the Euxine Sea. [...]

We shall begin our description by taking the oceans in regular order, first with the waters of the Atlantic, which Cadiz made famous by Hercules' gift of the pillar, where Atlas, standing on the mountain, holds up the columns that support the heavens above the earth. The first sea is the Iberian, which separates Europe from Libya and washes up on the shores of both. On either side of the sea are the pillars.[75] Both columns face the shores, one looking toward Europe and the other toward Libya. Next we come to the Gallic Sea whose waves strike the Celtic shores. If we continue to follow the coast of this sea, called by the name of the Lingurians, where the masters of the world grew on Latin soil, it extends north to Leucopetra where the island of Sicily with its curving shores makes a strait. Cyrnos[76] is washed by the waters that bear this name and that flow between the Sardinian Sea and the Celtic Sea. Next roll the long tides of the Tyrrhenian Sea, turning toward the south. This sea enters the sea of Sicily, which turns eastward and spreads far from the shores of Pachynum extending to Crete, a steep rocky cliff, which stands out from the sea and where the powerful Gortyna and Phaestum[77] are found in the midst of its fields. This island resembles with its peaks the forehead of a ram that the Greeks have correctly called *Criou metopon*. The sea of Sicily ends at Mount Garganus[78] on the coast of Apulia.

Beginning at that point the vast Adriatic extends in the direction of the northwest. There is also the Ionian Sea, famous throughout the world. The sea separates two shores that are seen to meet in one point. On the right, fertile Illyria[79] extends to the land of the warlike Dalmatians. The left is bounded by the Ausonian[80] peninsula, its curving shores touching three seas, the Tyrrhenian, the vast Adriatic, and the Sicilian, and encircle it on all sides. Each of these seas has winds within its limits that are original to it. The west wind lashes the Tyrrhenian, the south wind the Sicilian and the east wind breaks the waters of the Adriatic, the waves of which roll beneath its gusts.

Leaving Sicily, the sea increases its deep expanse to the greater Syrtis,[81] which the coast of Libya encircles. After the greater Syrtis passes into the lesser,[82] the two seas spread far and wide upon the rebounding shores. From Sicily the Cretan Sea stretches out toward the east as far as Salmonis, which is said to be the eastern end of Crete.

Next come two vast seas with dark waves, lashed by the north wind coming from Ismarus,[83] which rushes straight down from the regions of the north. The first, called the Pharian Sea, washes the base of steep mountain. The second is the Sidonian Sea, which turns toward the north joining there the Gulf of Issus. This sea does not extend far in a straight line but is broken by the shores of Cilicia. Then bending westward, it winds like a large dragon forcing its way through the mountains devastating the hills and the forests. Its end binds Pamphylia and surrounds the Chelidonian cliffs. Far off in the west it ends near the heights of Patara.[84]

Next we look again toward the north and find the Aegean Sea, whose waves exceed those of all other seas, and whose vast extent surrounds the scattered Cyclades. It ends near Imbros[85] and Tenedos, near the narrow straight through which the waters of the Propontis[86] issue, beyond which Asia with its many peoples extends to the south, where a wide peninsula unfolds. Then comes the Thracian Bosphorous, the mouth of the Black Sea. In the entire world many say that there is no strait narrower than this. On one of the two sides there are found the Symplegades,[87] close together. From there to the east the Black Sea spreads out aligning itself to the northeast. In the middle of the waters from each side juts out a promontory. The first, coming from Asia on the south side, is called the Carambis. The other from the opposite side juts out from the continent of Europe and is called the ram's forehead. These promontories face each other and are separated by a wide expanse of sea that takes three days to cross. Thus the Black Sea appears as a double sea that resembles the curve of a bow when the string is drawn. The right side of the sea is straight, and outside of the line forming the string is found Carambis projecting toward the north. The coast that encloses the sea on the left side makes two turns and is as the bow. Into this sea toward the north Lake Maeotis[88] enters and is enclosed on all sides by the land of the Scythians, who call Lake Maeotis the mother of the sea. At this location the violent sea flows in a great stream rushing across the Cimmerian Bosphorus in the coldest regions where the Cimmerians live at the base of Taurus.[89] Such is the picture of the oceans and the shining appearance of the deep.

As we have said previously, the sea is full of islands, the most important of which Ptolemy says are the following: Taprobane, in the Indian Ocean below the equator; Albion, also called Britain; Sardinia, in the Mediterranean Sea; Candia, also called Crete, in the Aegean; Selandia; Sicily; Corsica and Cyprus.

Unknown to Ptolemy are Madagascar, in the Prasodes Sea; Zanzibar; Java, in the east Indian Ocean; Angama; Peuta, in the Indian Ocean; Zipangi in the western Ocean. Of these Priscian says:

These are large islands which the waters of the ocean surround. There are many other islands that are much smaller, scattered about in various parts of the world, many that are unknown and that are difficult to sail to by sailors or unsuitable for ports. Their names I cannot simply express in verse.[90]

To determine the exact distance from one place to another, the elevation of the pole is something that must be considered. We shall briefly state therefore that, as has

Prolo‧quium.

gionū & locorū ab æquatore distantiā demõstrat. Est em tantus loci tractus ab æquatore cuius mē‧surā scire desideras /quãta ē eleuatio poli ad zenith eiusdē. Ex quibus milliariū numerus facilis cogni‧tu euadit/dū eundē p numerū eleuatiõis poli multi‧plicaueris. Verū tñ nõ sunt secudū Ptholomēi sen‧tentiā milliaria a circulo ēqnõctiali ad Arcton vbi cȝ gētiū æquales. Nã a primo æquatoris gradu vscȝ ad duodecimū/qlibet graduū sexaginta Italica mil‧liaria cõtinet quę faciūt.15 Germanica. Cõmuniter em quatuor Italica pro vno Germanico reputāt. Et a.12.gradu vscȝ ad.25.quilibet.59. milliaria facit quę sunt Germanis.12.½.¾. Atcȝ vt res fiat apertior ponemus formulam sequentem.

	Gradus	Gradus	Millia Ital.	Mil. Ger
Aequator.	1	12	60	15
	12	25	59	14 ½ ¼
Tropicus.	25	30	54	13 ½
	30	31	50	12 ½
	31	41	45	11 ¼
	41 usȝ ad	51 faciunt	40	10
	51	57	32	8
	57	63	28	7
	63	66	26	6 ½
Circu. Arcti.	66	70	21	5 ¼
	70	80	6	1 ½
Polus Arcti.	80	90		0

been made clear by what we said before, both poles are in the horizon for those who inhabit the parallel that is the equator. As one moves toward the north, however, the elevation of the pole increases the farther one moves away from the equator. The elevation of the pole indicates the distance of places from that parallel, for the distance of any place from the equator varies as the elevation of the pole from that place. The number of miles at each of these elevations is easy to ascertain by multiplying the number of degrees of elevation of the pole. According to Ptolemy the miles are not equal from the equator to the Arctic pole in all parts of the world. For any one of the degrees from the first degree of the equator up to the twelfth contains 60 Italian miles, which are equivalent in size to 15 German miles, four Italian miles being about equal to one German mile. Any degree from the twelfth degree up to the 25th contains 59 miles, or 14¾ German miles. So that these matters can be understood in an easier fashion we have inserted the following table (figure 6[91]).

In like manner, from the equator to either the Arctic or Antarctic pole, the number of miles in the degree of latitude varies. Should you wish to find the number of miles between one place and another, examine carefully in what degree of latitude the two places are and how many degrees there are between them. Using the above table, find out how many miles there are in a degree of that kind and multiply this number by the number of degrees between the places.[92] To convert these from Italian to German miles you will have to divide by four.

All that we have said here in our Introduction to Cosmography will provide sufficient understanding only if we tell you that in designing the layout of our world map we have not been faithful to Ptolemy in every respect, particularly in the layout of the new lands, where on the nautical charts we find that the equator has been placed differently than Ptolemy represented it. Therefore when you see this do not think it is our mistake, for we have represented it this way purposely, because at times we have followed Ptolemy and at other times the nautical charts. Ptolemy himself, in the fifth chapter of the first book of his *Cosmographia,* says that he did not have complete knowledge of all parts of the continent because of its enormous size and the inaccuracy of travelers' reports, that were not correctly handed down through their writings and tales, and that there are other parts of the world that are different now from what they were before or have ceased to exist owing to some cataclysm. For us, therefore, it has been necessary, as Ptolemy himself suggests, to place more faith in the information gathered in our times. We have on our map therefore followed Ptolemy, added new lands and some other things, while on the globe, which we have made to accompany the map, we have followed the description of Amerigo.

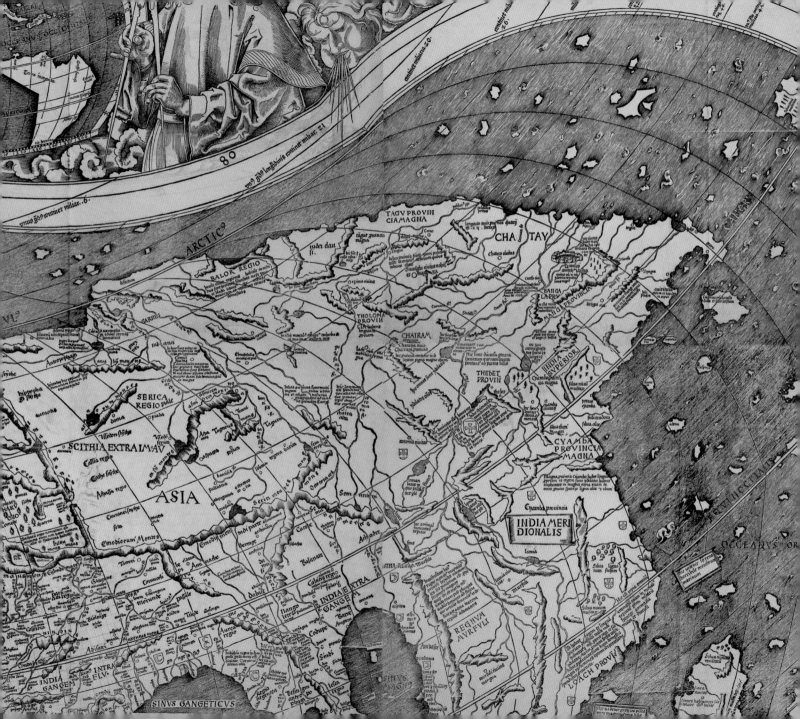

Appendix: Translation of Text Block on Verso of Schematic Map in Chapter 8[93]

The reason for this little book is to put forth a certain kind of introduction to our description of the universe drawn both as a globe and as a map. The globe I have made small, while the map is larger. As farmers divide their land and mark off boundaries in their fields, so it has been our purpose here to delineate the most important parts of the world by the symbols of their rulers. Beginning with our continent and in the middle of Europe we have placed the Eagles of the Holy Roman Empire with the key that is the symbol of our Holy Father. Using these symbols we have enclosed almost the whole of Europe for the Roman Church. The larger part of Africa and a particular part of Asia we have distinguished with the crescent of the supreme Sultan of Babylonia, the lord of all of Egypt and the ruler of part of Asia. We have surrounded Asia Minor with the saffron-colored cross along with an iron that is the symbol of the Sultan of the Turks. The Sultan rules Scythia this side of Imaus, the highest of the mountains of Asia and Sarmatian Scythia. In Asiatic Scythia we have drawn the anchors that are a symbol of the Great Tartar Khan. A red cross symbolizes the lands of Prester John, who rules all of Southern India and who makes his home in Biberith. Finally, on the fourth division of the earth, discovered by the Kings of Castile and Portugal, we have placed the emblems of those rulers. We have also placed small crosses in shallow places and areas where care must be exercised and shipwreck may be feared. With this we end.

Notes and References

1 A poem of two verses consisting of a hexameter and a pentameter.

2 Emperor Maximilian I (1459–1519) of the House of Habsburg. He was not given the title Holy Roman Emperor until 1508.

3 This is the hellenized name of Matthias Ringmann.

4 This is the hellenized name of Martin Waldseemüller.

5 Apollonius of Tyana was a neo-Pythagorean philosopher of the first century AD. His travels are best known through the work of Philostratus whose biography of him is built upon a series of dialogues. He is reported to have traveled to India and around South Asia.

6 Waldseemüller is apparently making a case for learning geography through studying the books and maps of others rather than through travel. Later in the *Introductio* he will quote extensively from the Latin translation of Priscian of the *Periegetes* of Dionysius. In that text Dionysius says that he does not "dwell in dark ships, or follow the profession of the merchant, or traverse divers lands" but instead his geography is taken from books and is guided by the muses to inform the minds of men.

7 Boethius, *Consolation of Philosophy*, 2.6.10–15.

8 Homer, *Odyssey*, 1.1–3.

9 See Introduction for description of the manuscript and Waldseemüller's correspondence with Johannes Amerbach.

10 The *Sphere*, capitulum 1, quotes Theodosius: *Sphaera vero a Theodosio sic describitur: sphaera est corpus solidum una superficie contentum in cuius medio punctus est a quo omnes lineae ductae ad circumferentiam sunt equales, et ille punctus dicitur centrum sphaerae* ("By Theodosius a sphere is described thus: A sphere is a solid body contained within a single surface, in the middle of which there is a point from which all straight lines drawn to the circumference are equal, and that point is called the "center of the sphere.")

11 Theodosius (ca. 100 BC) was the author of the *Sphaerica,* a book on the geometry of the sphere, written to provide a mathematical background for astronomy. It is thought that *Sphaerica* is based on some pre-Euclidean textbook which is now lost. Theodosius defines a sphere to be a solid figure with the property that any point on its surface is at a constant distance from a fixed point (the center of the sphere). He gives theorems that generalize those given by Euclid in Book III of the *Elements* for the circle.

12 The quote is from Manilius, *Astronomicon*, 1.279–81:

Aera per gelidum tenuis deducitur axis
libratumque regit diverso cardine mundum,
sidereus circa medium quem volvitur orbis.

Waldseemüller drops a line of the text in his quotation. The first printed edition of the *Astronomicon* was prepared by the astronomer Regiomontanus using very corrupted manuscripts, and published in 1473.

13 *Cardines* pertains to door hinges but is also used as "that on which something turns."

14 Note similarities with the *Sphere* (capitulum 2), where Waldseemüller uses the same Virgil quote at the end of his explanation: "It is to be noted that the pole which always is visible to us is called 'septentrional,' 'arctic,' or 'boreal.' 'Septentrional' is from *septentrio*, that is, from Ursa Minor, which is derived from *septem* and *trion*, meaning 'ox,' because the seven stars in Ursa move slowly, since they are near the pole. Those seven stars are also called *septentriones* as if *septem teriones*, because they tread the parts about the pole. 'Arctic' is derived from *arthos*, which is Ursa Major, for it is near Ursa Major. It is called 'boreal' because it is where the wind Boreas comes from. The opposite pole is called 'Antarctic' as opposed to 'Arctic.' It also is called 'meridional' because it is to the south, and it is called 'austral' because it is where the wind Auster comes from. The two fixed points in the firmament are called the 'poles of the world' because they terminate the axis of the sphere and the world revolves on them. One of these poles is always visible to us, the other always hidden. Whence Virgil: 'One pole is ever high above us while the other, beneath our feet is seen of black Styx and shades infernal.'"

15 Virgil, *Georgics*, 1.242–43.

16 *Plaustrum* (usually plural *Plaustra*) is the Latin for the constellation of the Great Bear or Ursa Major.

17 The constellation of Ursa Minor, meaning

Little Bear in Latin, is commonly called the Little Dipper. It is much less conspicuous than the Big Dipper, but it contains the most important navigational star, Polaris, the Pole or North Star.

18 Baptista Spagnuoli Mantuanus (1448–1516) was a Carmelite monk and poet. Mantuan's most notable works in prose include *De Patientia*, a rambling discourse on physical and spiritual illness that includes an early allusion to Columbus' discovery of America, and *De Vita Beata*, a dialogue on the religious life that he wrote soon after entering the Carmelite order. He is also known for his *Opus Aureum in Thomistas*, an early humanist critique of the late medieval philosophy and theology associated with Thomas Aquinas. His most important work and the one quoted here is his *Eclogues* published in the style of Virgil.

19 *Sphere, capitulum*[2]: *Horum autem circulorum quidam sunt maiores, quidam minores, ut sensui patet.* ("Of these circles some are larger, some smaller, as sense shows.")

20 *Sphere*: "There is another circle in the sphere which intersects the equinoctial and is intersected by it into two equal parts. One half of it tips toward the north, the other toward the south. That circle is called 'zodiac' from *zoe*, meaning 'life,' because all life in inferior things depends on the movement of the planets beneath it. Or it is derived from *zodias*, which means 'animal,' because, since it is divided into twelve equal parts, each part is called a sign and has its particular name from the name of some animal, because of

some property characteristic of it and of the animal, or because of the arrangement of the fixed stars there in the outline of that kind of animal. That circle in Latin is called *signifer* because it bears the 'signs' or because it is divided into them."

21 Aristotle in *On Generation and Corruption* calls it the "oblique circle," where he says that, according to the access and recess of the sun in the oblique circle, "are produced generations and corruptions in things below." In the early 16th century the framework for the study of natural phenomena was provided by Aristotle's *libri naturales* consisting of his books the *Physics, De Caelo, On Generation and Corruption, Meteorology, De Anima* and the *Parva Naturalia* along with their associated commentaries. The scholarship on Renaissance Aristotle commentaries is still in its infancy. In no other period of the history of philosophy have so many commentaries on works by Aristotle been written (both per year and in total) as in the Renaissance. Even on the incomplete basis of Lohr's first version of his catalogue of Renaissance Latin Aristotle Commentaries, Richard Blum has counted 6,653 such commentaries for the period 1500 to 1650. Charles Lohr's listing of commentaries can be found in *Renaissance Quarterly*, 1974 through 1988, and for analysis see Richard Blum's "Der standardkursus der katholischen Schulphilosophie in 17 Jahrhundert," in *Aristotelismus und Renaissance: In memorium Charles B. Schmitt* (Wiesbaden: Otto Harassowitz, 1988), 127–148. For more on this subject generally, see Charles B.

Schmitt, *Aristotle in the Renaissance*, The Martin Classical Lectures (Cambridge, Mass.: Harvard University Press, 1983).

22 *Sphere*: "The line dividing the zodiac in its circuit, so that on one side it leaves 6 degrees and on the other side another 6, is called the 'ecliptic,' since when sun and moon are on that line there occurs an eclipse of sun or moon. The sun always moves beneath the ecliptic, but all the other planets decline toward north or south; sometimes, however, they are beneath the ecliptic."

23 *Sphere*: "There are two other great circles in the sphere which are called 'colures,' whose function is to distinguish solstices and equinoxes. 'Colure' is derived from *colon*, which is a member, and *ouros*, which is a wild ox, because, just as the lifted tail of the wild ox, which is its member, describes a semicircle and not a complete circle, so a colure always appears to us imperfect because only one half of it is seen."

24 In 1508 Matthias Ringmann made the first translation of the Commentaries of Julius Caesar from Latin into German. The text was printed by Johannes Gruninger in Strasbourg under the title *Julius der erste romisch Kaiser von seinem Leben und Krieg.*

25 In the *Almagest* Ptolemy says that the earth is so small in relation to the size of the celestial sphere that the horizon plane seems to divide that sphere into two exactly equal parts. The horizon is therefore another great circle but according to Ptolemy does not rotate because the earth itself is fixed. The horizon is therefore unique to a particular locality and makes a par-

ticular angle of inclination with the axis of rotation of the celestial sphere. See G.J. Toomer's translation, *Ptolemy's Almagest* (Princeton: Princeton University Press, 1998), 43.

26 Waldseemüller uses "primum mobile," which is defined as the outermost concentric sphere of the universe, thought in Ptolemaic astronomy to revolve around the earth from east to west in 24 hours and believed to cause the other spheres to revolve with it. The concept of a transcendent prime mover as the cause of all motion in the universe was a controversial one in Waldseemüller's time as discussions of motion melded both Platonic and Aristotelean theories in many popular commentaries. In the *De Caelo,* for example, Aristotle has many passages that both imply and exclude the possibility of a prime mover. See Leo Elders' *Aristotle's Cosmology: A Commentary on the De Caelo* (Amsterdam: Van Gorcum, 1965), 27ff.

27 Virgil, *Georgics*, 1.233–40.

28 This is an error. Waldseemüller uses the correct value of 23°51′ later in the text.

29 Another error for 23°51′.

30 Waldseemüller is explaining how he rounded off the values of the distances of the various circles for a clearer presentation.

31 Ovid, *Metamorphoses*, 1.45–51.

32 *Sphere*: "That zone which lies between the tropics is said to be uninhabitable because of the heat of the sun, which ever courses between the tropics. Similarly, the zone of earth directly beneath it is said to be uninhabitable because of the intensity of the sun, which always courses above it. But those two zones, which are described by the Arctic Circle

and the Antarctic circle about the poles of the world, are uninhabitable because of too great cold, since the sun is far removed from them. The same is to be understood of the zones of earth directly beneath them. But those two zones of which one is between the summer tropic and the Arctic Circle and the other between the winter tropic and the Antarctic Circle are habitable and tempered from the heat of the torrid zone between the tropics and from the cold of the extreme zones which lie about the poles. The same is to be understood of the stretches of earth directly beneath them."

33 Chersonese is a name that was given to several different places in ancient times. Waldseemüller is using the name for what is now known as the Malay Peninsula.

34 This is the island of Sri Lanka but it was not always identified as such in the sixteenth century. Determining its size, shape, and exact position was a question from the earliest ages of classical geography and there had long been speculation among the ancient Greeks and the Romans as to whether Taprobane was a second world or whether it was a very great island. Strabo oriented it wrongly in the direction of Ethiopia and gave its length as over 5,000 stades, while Eratosthenes estimated the length of the island as equal to 8,000 stades. Repeating a similar misconception, the anonymous Greek sailor from Roman Egypt stated in the *Periplus Maris Erythraei* that Taprobane extended from the east to the west and that it was large enough to nearly reach the coast of Africa. Pomponius Mela, whom

Waldseemüller quotes from later in the text, was uncertain whether he should consider Taprobane a large island or the commencement of another world. Hipparchus saw it as a new hemisphere and the Elder Pliny observed that it was held to be another world and that it was discovered to be an island only in the age of Alexander the Great. Ptolemy depicted it as an island in the Indian Ocean of nearly continental size, making it 15 degrees wide and showing it on the final regional map of his *Geographia*. The name Taprobane was applied to Sumatra from the 15th century onwards. This occurred after a misunderstanding by the Italian traveller Niccolò di Conti. Conti was the first European traveller who distinguished Ceylon from Taprobane and identified the latter as Sumatra.

35 Waldseemüller describes a system of parallels very much like that of Ptolemy. The parallels in Ptolemy's *Geographia* were divided according to the length of the longest day at particular locations. This results in the uneven spacing of the parallels and sets the system apart from its modern counterparts where parallels generally are evenly spaced.

36 Almucantars are the circles of equal altitude projected onto the celestial sphere. They are small circles that, along with azimuths, produce a grid on the celestial sphere analogous to the grid produced by lines of longitude and latitude projected onto the earth.

37 Should read 42°18′.

38 It is important to note that the table gives a spacing between parallels that is Ptolemaic in structure and does not coincide with that

found on the 1507 World Map. This is the only place of significance in the *Cosmographiae Introductio* in which the text differs in any way from the 1507 map itself. Waldseemüller did, however, preserve the location of the Ptolemaic parallels on labels that appear in the map's border.

39 There is an error in the Table at parallel 18. The ½ that has been entered for the distance should be placed with the 17 in the hour column as 17½ .

40 It appears that Waldseemüller is referring to a seventh climate towards the south which, if it is symmetrical with the northern climates, would place this area below 52 degrees south near where his representation of South America ends in the 1507 map's border.

41 Waldseemüller shows these in the border of the 1507 World Map and they represent an independent system of parallels.

42 Juvenal, *Satires*, 10.168.

43 Virgil, *Georgics*, 1.30.

44 Pomponius Mela considered the earth as divided by the equator into two hemispheres, the northern and southern, and all those who inhabited one of these hemispheres were considered as antichthones to those of the other.

45 Pomponius Mela is unique among ancient geographers in that, after dividing the earth into five zones, of which only two were habitable, he asserts the existence of antichthones, inhabiting the southern temperate zone inaccessible to the people of the northern temperate regions because of the unbearable heat of the intervening torrid belt. The quote is from *De Situ Orbis*, 1.1.9: *Zonis quinque distinguitur.*

Mediam aestus infestat, frigus ultimas: reliquae habitabiles paria agunt anni tempora, verum non pariter. Antichthones alteram, nos alteram incolimus. Illius situs, ob ardorem intercedentis plagae, incognitus; huius dicendus est. Waldseemüller's source is the Erhard Ratdolt edition of 1482, printed in Venice.

46 Virgil, *Georgics*, 1.54–59.

47 Aristotle discusses winds extensively in his *Meteorology*. For example, "The explanation of these and many other phenomena is this. When the sun warms the earth the evaporation that takes place is necessarily of two kinds, not of one only as some think. One kind is rather of the nature of vapor, the other of the nature of a windy exhalation. That which rises from the moisture contained in the earth and on its surface is vapour, while that rising from the earth itself, which is dry, is like smoke. Of these the windy exhalation, being warm, rises above the moister vapor, which is heavy and sinks below the other. Hence the world surrounding the earth is ordered as follows." Another popular source for the names of the winds comes from a text that in the early 16th century was thought to be by Aristotle but is now know to be spurious. The text entitled *The Situations and Names of the Winds* is interesting in that it ends by describing a graphic element that is part of the border of almost every map of the period: "I have drawn for you a circle of the earth and indicated the positions of the winds, and the directions in which they blow, so that they may be presented to your vision." Waldseemüller, of course, places the

winds and their directions in the border of the 1507 World Map.

48 The directions of the winds are as follows: from the east, *Kaikias, Subsolanus, Eurus*; from the west, *Chorus, Zephyrus, Africanus*; from the south, *Euronotus, Aster (Notus), Libonotus*; from the north, *Septemtrio, Aquilo (Boreas), Trachias (Circius).*

49 Ovid, *Metamorphoses*, 1.61–66.

50 Virgil, *Georgics*, 1.44.

51 Ovid, *Metamorphoses*, 1.264.

52 Virgil, *Aeneid*, 3.285.

53 Name of Johannes Hänlein (1495–1525), a poet and contemporary of Waldseemüller. He was schoolmaster at Jung St. Peter's chapter school in Strasbourg in 1503 where he introduced humanist methods of instruction. In 1512 he taught rhetoric and grammar at the Sélestat grammar school in Alsace. He was a correspondent with Erasmus.

54 On the verso of this figure, which is a double-page foldout in the original 1507 editions, Waldseemüller has placed some text that appears to be misplaced. It does not flow with the rest of the text that follows and appears to be meant for an alternate introduction or description of the 1507 World Map. I translate this text as an Appendix.

55 Waldseemüller uses the Latin word *fere*. This is a difficult section of the text as the word implies the newly discovered fourth part of the world was partially known to Ptolemy.

56 The Tanais River flowed through eastern Scythia and emptied into the Palus Maeotis (Sea of Azov) in the northeastern corner of the Black Sea.

57 Raetia was a province of the Roman Empire, bounded on the west by the country of the Helvetii, on the east by Noricum, on the north by Vindelicia, and on the south by Cisalpine Gaul. It thus comprised the districts occupied in modern times by eastern and central Switzerland (containing the Upper Rhine and Lake Constance), southern Bavaria and the upper Danube, Voralberg, the greater part of Tirol, and part of Lombardy. The northern border of Raetia was part of the Limes Germanicus (the German Border), stretching for 166 km along the Danube.

58 A Roman province in northern Morocco around Tangier.

59 A Roman city in what is now Algeria.

60 Cyrenaica was a Roman province on the northern coast of Africa between Egypt and Numidia. The area is now the eastern part of the Mediterranean coast of Libya.

61 Derived from the Greek word *aphrike*, meaning "without cold." This was proposed by Leo Africanus (1488–1554), who suggested the Greek word *phrike* (meaning "cold and horror"), combined with the negating prefix "a-," thus indicating a land free of cold and horror. However, as the change of spelling from *ph* to *f* in Greek is datable to about the 10th century, it is unlikely that this is the origin. The real origin of the name is either derived from Egyptian or the Proto-Kordofanian word for beautiful or perfection.

62 Bithynia was a Roman province in the northwest of Asia Minor, adjoining the Propontis, the Thracian Bosphorus and the Euxine Sea (today Black Sea).

63 Galatia was an area in the highlands of central Anatolia in modern Turkey. Galatia was bounded on the north by Bithynia and Paphlagonia, on the east by Pontus, on the south by Lycaonia and Cappadocia, and on the west by the remainder of Phrygia.

64 Pamphylia was the region in the south of Asia Minor, between Lycia and Cilicia, extending from the Mediterranean to Mount Taurus (modern day Antalya province, Turkey). It was bounded on the north by Pisidia and was therefore a country of small extent, having a coastline of about 75 miles with a breadth of about 30 miles. Under the Roman administration the term Pamphylia was extended so as to include Pisidia and the whole tract to the frontiers of Phrygia and Lycaonia. In this wider sense it is employed by Ptolemy.

65 Cilicia was the name of a region, now known as Çukurova, on the southeastern coast of Asia Minor (modern Turkey), north of Cyprus.

66 Colchis was a nearly triangular ancient Georgian region. Now mostly the western part of Georgia, in Greek mythology it was the home of Aeëtes and Medea and the destination of the Argonauts. The ancient area is represented roughly by the present-day Georgian provinces of Mingrelia, Imereti, Guria, Ajaria, Svaneti, Racha, Abkhazia and Turkey's Rize Province and parts of Trabzon and Artvin provinces.

67 Hyrcania was the ancient name of Golestan, Mazandaran, Gilan and parts of Turkmenistan that were located within the Persian Empire by the Caspian Sea.

68 Waldseemüller's Latin is extremely important here. He seems to be implying that he has evidence for a passage under the New World. Interestingly, however, he does not show South America as being surrounded by water on the 1507 World Map. Rather, he extends the continent of South America into the border of the map. See John Hessler, "Warping Waldseemüller: A Phenomenological and Computational Study of the 1507 World Map," *Cartographica* 41 (2006), 101–13.

69 Many Greek and Roman geographers, including Strabo, Pomponius Mela and Priscian, held the one ocean theory. See E.H. Bunbury, *A History of Ancient Geography* (London: J. Murray, 1932).

70 Dionysius Periegetes was the author of a description of the habitable world in Greek hexameter verse (the *Periegesis*). His dates and his origins are not known, but he is believed to have been from Alexandria and to have flourished around the time of Hadrian, though some scholars put him as late as the end of the 3rd century AD. The book was paraphrased into Latin by Rufus Festus Avienus, and translated by the grammarian Priscian, who is the source of Waldseemüller's quote. See J. Oliver Thompson, *History of Ancient Geography* (Cambridge: Cambridge University Press, 1948).

71 Waldseemüller quotes extensively, almost 5 pages in the *Cosmographiae Introductio*, from the *Periegesis* (see Introduction).

72 The Arimaspi of northern Scythia, perhaps in the foothills of the Carpathians, were legendary to Greek writers and it was said they had

a single eye in the center of their foreheads. They were also said to steal gold from the griffins, causing battles between the two groups. All tales of their struggles with the gold-guarding griffins in the Hyperborean lands near the cave of Boreas, the North Wind (*Geskleithron*), had their origin in *Arimaspea*, the lost archaic poem of Aristeas of Proconnesus. Some details of the Arimaspi are reported by Herodotus and Strabo and in Pliny's *Natural History*.

73 Waldseemüller and Ringmann do not quote the full text here and throughout their long quotation. The ellipses in brackets indicate locations where Waldseemüller and Ringmann skip parts of the text.

74 Panchaea is the name of a fictional island, first mentioned by ancient Greek philosopher Euhemerus.

75 The Pillars of Hercules is the ancient name given to the promontories that flank the entrance to the Strait of Gibraltar. The name derives from the story that after killing Medusa, Perseus took the head of the Gorgon with him to distant lands and reached the western end of the Earth where the sun sets. This is the land where Atlas resided and his nymph daughters the Hesperides raised magical golden apples in a lively garden filled with flowers. Perseus wished to rest in Atlas' daughters' garden and asked him for food, but Atlas – fearing that the hero would steal his magical fruit (not to mention his daughters) – refused and sent Perseus away. Perseus then showed Atlas the head of Medusa and the Titan turned into a giant.

His hair turned to wood and sprouted green leaves at the tips, and it grew and grew until it was a great forest of trees. His shoulders expanded into enormous cliffs and his bones into solid rock. Soon, his whole being was transformed into a mountain. It was believed that he continued to hold up the Earth even when he turned to stone.

76 The island of Corsica.

77 Ancient cities on Crete.

78 Monte Gargano is a mountain in Apulia, forming the backbone of the peninsula Promontorio del Gargano on the Adriatic Sea.

79 Illyria was a region in the western part of today's Balkan Peninsula

80 Ausonia is a Greek and Virgilian poetical name for Italy recalling the territory of the Ausones, a tribe of southern Italy.

81 Gulf of Sidra is a body of water in the Mediterranean Sea on the northern coast of Libya; it is also known as Gulf of Sirte. It is located by the city of Sirte.

82 The Gulf of Gabès, called Minor Syrtis in ancient times, is a gulf on Tunisia's east coast in the Mediterranean Sea. The gulf is 64 miles long and wide, with the Kerkena Islands on the northeast and Djerba Island on the southeast.

83 Ismara (or *Ismaros*) is an ancient Ciconian town on the Aegean coast of Thrace and supposedly was the city mentioned in the *Odyssey*.

84 Patara was later renamed Arsinoe and was a flourishing maritime and commercial city on the southwest coast of Lycia on the Mediterranean coast of Turkey near the modern

small town of Gelemi, in Antalya Province.

85 Imbros, known as Gökçeada, is the largest island of Turkey, part of Çanakkale Province. It is located at the entrance of Saros Bay in the northern Aegean Sea.

86 Propontis was the ancient Greek name for the sea also known as the Sea of Marmora. It connects the Black Sea to the Aegean Sea.

87 In Greek mythology, the Symplegades were a pair of rocks at the Hellespont that clashed together randomly.

88 This is the Sea of Azov, a northern section of the Black Sea linked to the larger body through the Strait of Kerch. It is bounded on the north by Ukraine, on the east by Russia and on the west by the Crimean peninsula.

89 The Tauri were a people settling on the southern coast of the Crimean peninsula, inhabiting the Crimean Mountains and the narrow strip of land between the mountains and the Black Sea. They gave their name to the peninsula, which was known in ancient times as *Taurica*, *Taurida* and *Tauris*.

90 Priscian, *Periegesis*, 609–13.

91 Waldseemüller's figures for the distances in miles along any parallel are fairly accurate even though he seems to be implying that the changes in distance are discrete and not continuous. A graph that compares his distances with modern values can be found in John Hessler, "Warping Waldseemüller: A Phenomenological and Computational Study of the 1507 World Map," *Cartographica* 41 (2006), 101–13.

92 This methodology works only with places that are on the same parallel. Ptolemy ex-

plains in greater detail how to determine the distance between two places on the surface of the earth. Ptolemy's methods often involve many steps and it is not apparent how much spherical geometry Waldseemüller knew from Ptolemy. For more on this, see Lennart Berggren and Alexander Jones, *Ptolemy's Geography: An Annotated Translation of the Theoretical Chapters* (Princeton: Princeton University Press, 2000), 16–17.

93 This text insert talks about the coloration of the flags on the 1507 map. The only color evident, however, on the LOC copy was put there by Schöner and consists of red lines drawn in the form of a grid over particular regions and of red colored circles at certain city locations.

Further Reading

Although the bibliography of articles and books on the early mapping of America is large, there are actually few studies specifically dedicated to the Waldseemüller maps. The following bibliography provides suggestions for further reading on various subjects concerning Waldseemüller and his time.

Primary Sources

Copia der Newen Zeytung aus Pressillg Landt, Tidings out of Brazil, reproduced and translated with commentary by M. Graubard and J. Parker (Minneapolis: University of Minnesota Press, 1957).

Amerbach, Johann. *The Correspondence of Johann Amerbach: Early Printing in its Social Context*, trans. Barbara C. Halporn (Ann Arbor: University of Michigan Press, 2000).

D'Avezac-Macaya, Marie Armand Pascal. *Hylacomylus Waltzemuller, ses ouvrages et ses collaborateurs* (Paris: Challamel Aine, 1867).

Ludd, Galthius. *Speculi Orbis succincta declaratio* (Strasbourg: J. Gruninger, 1507).

Schöner, Johannes. *Luculentissima quaedam terrae totius descriptio* (Nuremberg: Johannes Stuchssen, 1515).

Trithemius, Johannes. *Epistularum Familarium* (Hagenau, 1536).

Vespucci, Amerigo. *Letter to Piero Soderini,* edited and translated by George Tyler Northup (Princeton: Princeton University Press, 1916).

Werner, Johannes. *Libellus de quator tarrarum orbis in plano figurationibus* (Nuremberg: Joannes Stucjs, 1514).

Werner, Johannes. *Canones sicut brevissimi, ita etiam doctissimi, complectentes praecepta et observations de mutatione aurae* (Nuremberg: Joannes Montanus and Ulrichus Neuber, 1546).

Waldseemüller, Martin and Matthias Ringmann. *Cosmographiae Introductio …, Rudimenta* (St. Dié, 1507). Reprinted by Joseph Fischer and Franz von Wieser, *The Cosmographiae Introductio of Martin Waldseemuller in facsimile, followed by the Four Voyages of Amerigo Vespucci, with their Translation into English; to which are added Waldseemuller's two maps of 1507 with an Introduction*, ed. Charles George Hebermann (New York: United States Catholic Historical Society, 1907).

On Ptolemy

Ptolemy, Claudius. *Ptolemy's Geography: An Annotated Translation of the Theoretical Chapters*, trans. J. Lennart Berggren and Alexander Jones (Princeton: Princeton University Press, 2000).

Diller, Aubrey. "The Parallels on Ptolemaic Maps," *Isis* 33 (1941), 4–7.

Stahl, William Harris. "Ptolemy's Geography: A Select Bibliography," *Bulletin of the New York Public Library* 55.9 (1951), 419–432.

On Waldseemuller

Harris, Elizabeth. "The Waldseemüller World Map: A Typographic Appraisal," *Imago Mundi* 37 (1985), 30–53.

Herbermann, Charles G. "The Waldseemüller Map of 1507," *Historical Records and Studies* 3 (1904), 320–342.

Hessler, John. "Warping Waldseemuller: A Cartometric Study of the Coast of South America as Portrayed on the 1507 World Map." *Coordinates*, Series A (2005). http://www.sunsb.edu/libmap/coordinates/contents.ttml

_____. "Warping Waldseemüller: A Phenonmenological and Computational Study of the 1507 World Map," *Cartographica* 44 (2006) 101–113.

_____. "Warping Waldseemüller: Mathematical Methods in Historical Cartometry," weblog located at http://www.warpinghistory.blogspot.com.

Johnson, Christine R. "Renaissance German Cosmographers and the Naming of America," *Past & Present* 191 (2006), 3–43.

Karrow, Robert W. *Mapmakers of the Sixteenth Century and their Maps: Bio-Bibliographies of the*

Cartographers of Abraham Ortelius, 1570 (Chicago: Speculum Orbis Press, 1993), 568–583.

Laubenberger, Franz. "The Naming of America," *Sixteenth Century Journal* 13.4 (1982), 91–113.

Schwartz, Seymour. *Putting America on the Map*, (New York: Prometheus Press, 2007).

On Schöner and German Humanism
Chrisman, Miriam. *Lay Culture, Learned Culture: Books and Social Change in Strasburg 1480–1599* (New Haven: Yale University Press, 1982).

Brann, Noel. *The Abbot Trithemius (1462–1516): The Renaissance of Monastic Humanism* (Leiden: E.J. Brill, 1981).

Broeckes, Steven Vanden. *The Limits of Influence: Pico, Louvain, and the Crisis of Renaissance Astrology* (Lieden: E.J. Brill, 2003).

Coote, Charles Henry. *Johann Schöner, Professor of Mathematics at Nuremberg, a Reproduction of his Globe of 1523, Long Lost, his Dedicatory Letter to Reymer von Streytperck, and the 'De Molvccis' of Maximilianus Transylvanus* (London: H. Stevens, 1888), 149–168.

Durand, Dana Bennett. *The Vienna-Klosterneuberg Map Corpus of the Fifteenth Century: A Study in the Transition from Medieval to Modern Science* (Leiden: E.J. Brill, 1952).

Field, Judith Veronica. *The Invention of Infinity:*

Mathematics and Art in the Renaissance (New York: Oxford University Press, 1997).

Gallois, Lucien. *Les Géographes allemands de la Renaissance* (Paris: E. Leroux, 1890; Amsterdam: Meridian Publishing, 1963), 70–97.

Grafton, Anthony. *Joseph Scaliger: A Study in the History of Classical Scholarship* (Oxford: Oxford University Press, 1983).

Klemm, Hans Gunther. *Die fränkische Mathematicus Johann Schöner (1477-1547) und seine kirchehrenbacher Briefe an den nürnberger Patrizier Willibald Pirckheimer* (Forchheim: Ehrenbürg-Gymnasium, 1992).

Reicke, Emil. "Aus dem Leben des Johann Schöner, ersten Professors für Mathematik und Geographie in Nürnberg," *Abhandlungen der Naturhistorischen Gesellschaft Nürnberg* 17 (1907), 41–59.

Schmitt, Charles. *Aristotle in the Renaissance*, Mass. (Cambridge: Harvard University Press, 1983).

INDIA MERIDIONALIS

Cyamba prouincia

OCCEANVS ORIENTALIS INDICVS

REGNVM AVREVM

LOACH PROVI

SINVS MAGNVS

INDIAE EXTRA GANGEM

CANDIH

IAVA MAIOR

ZOABAR PROVINCIA

INDIA

REGNVM VARR

CAPRICORNII

NECVRA

ANGAMA

PELTAM

CAPRICORNII

WLTVRN9 EVRVS

GANGETICVS

Balacham

OLACCIVS

LAC REGINA

SEYLAM

IAVA MINOR

EVRONOTVS

Callen zuam

IAO   180   190   200   210   220   230   240   250   260   270

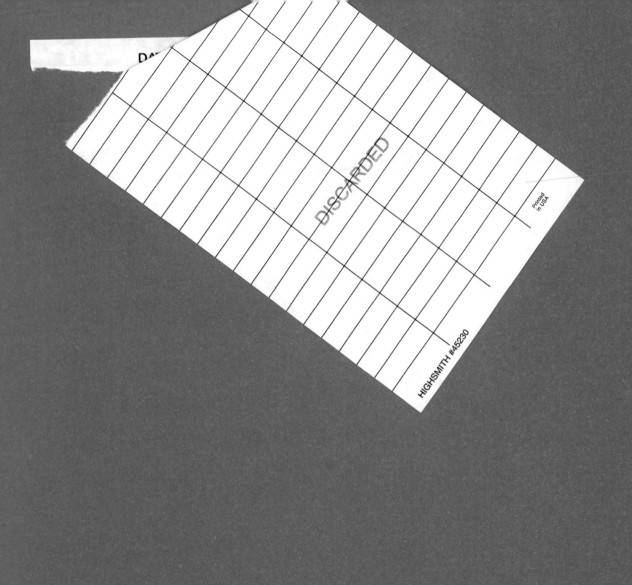

DISCARDED